The Significant Lawyer

MERCER UNIVERSITY PRESS

Endowed by

TOM WATSON BROWN
and
THE WATSON-BROWN FOUNDATION, INC.

The Significant Lawyer

The Pursuit of Purpose and Professionalism

WILLIAM S. DUFFEY JR.

MERCER UNIVERSITY PRESS

Macon, Georgia

MUP/ H1016

© 2022 by William S. Duffey Jr.
Published by Mercer University Press
1501 Mercer University Drive
Macon, Georgia 31207
All rights reserved

25 24 23 22 21   5 4 3 2 1

Books published by Mercer University Press are printed on acid-
free paper that meets the requirements of the American National
Standard for Information Sciences—Permanence of Paper for
Printed Library Materials.

Printed and bound in Canada.

This book is set in Adobe Caslon Pro.

Cover/jacket design by Burt&Burt.

ISBN   978-0-88146-820-5
Cataloging-in-Publication Data is available from the Library of Congress

For Betsy,

from the plateau of Anatolia to the rushing

water of the Soque, we have lived life fulfilled.

Contents

The Significant Lawyer

Introduction

"For lawyers, the obligation of professionalism includes conducting oneself in such a way as to honor the
legal profession.

"There is no better way to honor the profession than
in honorable conduct whether in practice or expanded areas of public service. In my opinion, honorable service is
the highest conduct of a lawyer."

—Griffin B. Bell
Former attorney general of the United States,
United States circuit judge, and lawyer

Griffin B. Bell was one of America's most accomplished and respected lawyers, with sincerely and firmly held views about the
legal profession. In 2008, shortly before he died, he wrote an
essay entitled "The Values of Our Profession."[1] In it, he ex-
pressed his belief that lawyers should honor their careers by engaging in honorable conduct. To him, the practice of law was
collegial. Truth and fairness were paramount, and lawyers cooperated in exchanging information about their cases, scheduling
events, and working with the court. Their word was their bond.
He often lamented, "We were trial lawyers back then. When you
called someone's assistant, they'd tell you their boss was in court.
Now you call them, and they tell you their boss is in a deposition.
We call it litigation." As he saw it, trials were a search for true
and fair results. Litigation was a process to leverage a settlement.

---

[1] *A Life in the Law: Advice for Young Lawyers*, eds. William S.
Duffey Jr. and Richard A. Schneider (ABA, 2009).

Today many lawyers don't see the practice of law as Judge Bell did. They view it simply as a business, not professionals seeking just results. As this "law as business" view has taken hold—a view I'll discuss in chapter 1—lawyers have become more prone to reject the authority of a court, engage in uncivil conduct toward colleagues, mistreat lawyers and staff, disrespect rights granted to citizens, and act in shameless self-promotion. Maybe there is a reason lawyers are the brunt of so many jokes.

Many in the profession regret this shift toward legal commercialism. Some began practicing at a time when lawyers were held in high esteem, and reveled in the robust advocacy of fact and legal issues. They've acted honestly and civilly without ever sacrificing their obligation to zealously and ethically represent their clients. Many of these attorneys also have done their level best to mentor and influence younger lawyers. Unfortunately, market forces now seem to conspire against them.

Like their predecessors, many of today's young lawyers enter the practice of law believing in the high ideals of the profession and having strongly held personal values. Over time, though, they find themselves influenced by those who say the lofty ideals of the profession must give way to practical considerations, namely, prioritizing profits. After all, their managing partner over their shoulder says that success is measured by the time you bill and the money you make. As a result, many young lawyers find law practice is not what they expected, or wanted. Still, they may sense there is a way to practice that is both fulfilling and provides a comfortable living. Are they right? Yes. How can they go about it? That's what this book is about.

Abraham Lincoln, who began his professional life as a lawyer, saw his entire career through a different lens. Whether serving as an attorney representing clients or serving the citizens of the United States as president, he saw his work as an extension of his ideals. Leo Tolstoy said of him:

INTRODUCTION

Of all the great national heroes and statesmen of history,
Lincoln is the only real giant. Alexander the Great, Cae-
sar, Napoleon, Gladstone, and even Washington stand in
greatness of character, in depth of feeling and in a certain
moral power far behind Lincoln.... However, the highest
heroism is that which is based on humanity, truth, justice
and pity; all other forms are doomed to forgetfulness....
Lincoln is a strong type of those who make for truth and
justice, for brotherhood and freedom. Love is the foundation of his life. That is what makes him immortal and
that is the quality of a giant.[2]

Lincoln's life was rooted in the virtues he held true. Virtu-
ous practice is not an outdated idea. In fact, as we'll recall in the
later chapters of this book, when lawyers are admitted to practice
today, they promise to abide by the shared professional values
embedded in the oath they take. These oaths are not aspirational
statements. They are inviolate promises. But these are not the
only promises we ought to make before entering the practice of
law. We ought to consider the values that form the foundation
of our lives. We ought to promise to align our practice to them,
even when we're drawn away by the triumvirate of professional
temptations: money, power, and prestige. Lincoln was true to
his values first, and as a result, he earned more than enough
money, ascended to the highest office in the land, and is held in
high esteem by history.

In this book, I'll call us back to the nobility of our practice.
I'll ask you to reclaim the shared values of our profession, to define your personal values, and commit to living them out in your
practice. In other words, I'll call you to align your conduct, your
practice, to the oaths you swore and the values you hold. After
all, if there's anything I've learned in life, it's that this kind of

---

[2] *New York World*, February 7, 1909.

alignment provides true satisfaction and fulfilment, and it is possible for every one of us.

Practicing aligned is not some sophomoric ideal. It is current, relevant, and fundamental to our profession and to our satisfaction practicing it. This book is my attempt to explain what it means to be an aligned lawyer and how this affects the relationships lawyers have with clients, opposing lawyers, the court, colleagues, and those closest to you. Here, I'll offer a number of stories to illustrate the points I make in the pages that follow. These stories are gleaned from my forty-five years of private practice and public service in seven different positions. Though I've chosen not to use real names (except for a few exceptions), the identities are less important than the principles demonstrated in the stories. Pay close attention and see if you find yourself in some, and maybe many, of them.

Are you ready to gain a deeper understanding of alignment in the practice of law? If you are, let's get started. But before we do, let's begin with a simple question: how did so many of us get so lost?

Chapter 1

Lost Lawyers

"[W]e examined every major study of lawyers' job satisfaction appearing in social science journals, law reviews, and bar journals. What emerged was not a pretty picture—what we termed 'high paid misery.'"
—*Richard Delgado and Jean Stefancic,*
"Can Lawyers Find Happiness?"[1]

When Stu arrived, I walked into our reception area to greet him. He avoided eye contact when we shook hands. When he looked up to walk with me to my chambers, I noticed dark bags under his eyes and his furrowed brow. I closed my chambers door as we entered, and invited Stu to have a seat on my sofa.

Stu was a young lawyer in a mid-sized civil litigation firm. I knew parts of Stu's story from the friend who asked me to meet with him. He said Stu needed direction in his career, and within minutes of entering my chambers, that was clear. We exchanged a few pleasantries, and then I asked him how his practice was going. He looked up and said he was thinking about leaving his firm. He hated what he was doing. He felt pressured to bill hours but got little feedback on the quality of his work. So long as his billable hours were high, things were fine. It was "all about billable work," he said. In fact, things had gotten so bad he was finding it increasingly hard to get up in the morning. All of this

---

[1] *Syracuse Law Review* 58 (2007): 241, 247.

was taking a toll on his marriage and his health. He paused, drew a deep breath, then looked up.

"I'm lost," he said. And I just nodded.

His story was not unique. I'd heard it dozens of times.

John called one evening to tell me he'd been offered a two-year policy position in a cabinet-level department in a presidential administration. A talented and highly compensated partner at a respected national firm, John wanted to know how I was able to move in and out of public service, how I handled the reduced pay in public service work, did I like government service, and did public service affect career options down the road. I addressed each of his questions, sensing he had strong interest in the job. Still, I didn't push him one way or the other.

As we ended our conversation, John told me he had always envied my courage to do different things professionally. He said he'd been with his firm for twenty years but felt he was in a professional wilderness, and had been for the past decade. He regretted not having more diverse legal practice experience. He was bored with the redundancy in his caseload, the rancor in private practice, and the sacrifice demanded by litigation work.

A couple of weeks later, John and I talked again, and I asked what he'd decided about the opportunity in Washington. He told me he'd decided to pursue the position, but after discussing it with his family, he bowed out. His wife and kids really liked having a husband and dad who was a partner in a prosperous law firm, and they didn't support his move to a new city and a government salary. Faced with this family response, he felt he had no other option. He resigned himself to his big-law practice, knowing he'd stay lost in his personal wilderness.

Small-firm attorneys have the same doubts about their practices. In my experience they have similar pressures, demands, and dissatisfaction.

Joann was a lawyer at a small, specialized firm that was in the middle of merger discussions with another firm. She didn't know how a merger might affect her position and wanted to discuss options if she lost her job. As we sifted through the possibilities, she wondered aloud whether it might be a good thing if she was let go, because she didn't like litigation and wanted more client- and transaction-oriented work. She felt lost in her small-firm, litigation-focused world—a confession she had never shared with anyone.

How a Profession Lost Its Way

"Lost," or some word like it, is often used by lawyers who ask to meet to discuss their careers. And though I don't keep a running tally of the lost lawyers with whom I've met, the number is large.

There are common themes among them. They are unhappy in their work. They grieve the focus on production and fee generation. Young lawyers mourn the absence of meaningful conversations with experienced lawyers. Older attorneys miss the more collaborative and collegial environments of their early years of practice. They all regret the loss of time to do things that bring balance to their life, time to develop meaningful relationships with colleagues and friends, and time to serve their families and communities. These are the common grievances of the lost.

Over the years, I've wondered how we lost our way as a profession. When I was invited as a young lawyer to join King & Spalding, a prestigious, large law firm in Atlanta, it was known as a practice of close-knit lawyers with high standards of excellence, strong prospects for advancement, and deep community connections. When I started with the firm, Richard Woodward, one of the firm's partners and a fellow South Carolinian, was assigned to help me transition to law practice. Richard's availability, willingness to set aside time from his demanding schedule, and wise counsel and openness all convinced me that he was invested in my success. He taught me the nuances of practice, the reality of firm politics, and how a strong work ethic was the key to doing well. He pointed to the list of the nonprofit boards on which the firm's lawyers served, including as board chairs. Volunteering our skills and talents, he said, was important to the firm's reputation, and it provided opportunities for us to showcase our superb legal work and judgment.

Richard always reminded me that the opportunities presented to us by the firm were the result of the vision and hard work of those who'd gone before us. King & Spalding, he told me, selected new partners from those who made their way up through the ranks and lived the values he described. If I contributed well, served clients well, lived well, advancement was relatively lockstep, as he put it. He didn't see that culture changing. But it did. King & Spalding, like many other firms, changed. Emphasis was placed on increasing revenues, looking for work that could be premium billed, and leveraging lawyer talent to increase billable hours. The business of law became the driving force.

People have offered various reasons for this business-focus pivot over the past couple of decades—a pivot that began, and which is most pronounced, in large-firm practice, but which has trickled down to, and now affects, firms of all sizes. In my experience, the evidence of this shift surfaced in the mid-eighties and was most obvious with the publication of *The American Lawyer 100* in 1986. This listing of the top one hundred law firms in America—at least as *The American Lawyer* saw it—invented a new performance matrix, ranking law firms by size and profitability. The list reported on a variety of fiscal measures. Until the 100 list was first published, information about law firm finances and profitability was apocryphal at best. Internal firm financial information was generally a closely held secret. There certainly was no clearinghouse detailing internal information about the financial performance of law firms. So, *The American Lawyer* legal magazine created one.

The publication of firm financial information captured the attention of lawyers across the country and, I suspect, sold a lot of subscriptions to the magazine. The information disclosed was specific and included firm size, annual gross revenues, number of lawyers, and the ratio of partners to associates. But the item that got the most attention was the calculation of profits per partner, or "PPP," as some lawyers liked to call it. It was the data point that allowed lawyers everywhere to see how much money partners were making at the one hundred top-grossing firms. Lawyers envied those doing well, and a new standard for success was established for those absent from the list. Whether your firm made the list or not, the values and culture of the profession began to shift as firms began to focus on PPP and lawyers began to chase it, including by considering marketing themselves and their practices to firms with higher PPP. Lawyers in private practice began to reconsider the purpose for practicing law. Was it really about justice, truth, service to clients, and the stature of the profession—the principal motivation that took them to law school in the first place—or was it about practical and measurable profitability targets? Was it about how much you could make in practice?

Within years, the pivot locked in. Profitability became a benchmark of success. It was a seductive success target because it was so objective. It was, after all, difficult, if not impossible, to compare firms based on their subjective accomplishments, such as the fairness of litigation results and transactions, client satisfaction with legal services, or the impact on conduct. Money was a much easier yardstick.

The Problem with Profit Comparisons

Like all businesses, profitability is the difference between gross revenues and expenses. And if you're reading this book, you probably understand that in law practice, revenues are based primarily on the total billable hours of lawyers and other professionals, multiplied by the hourly rate at which the hours are billed. And though the number of hours a lawyer can ethically bill are finite, firms can increase revenues by increasing the number of people who bill, or increasing hourly billing rates, or both. As firms sought to maximize profits by hiring attorneys to churn out more hours, even the nomenclature changed. In the late '80s, lawyers began referring to professionals as "billing units" or "headcount," a dehumanizing reference at best. And when the billing units or headcount wasn't high enough, revenues were increased by raising the required hours for associates or by upping hourly rates, often without a careful analysis of the impact of these increases on the quality of service, value to clients, or the satisfaction of lawyers, especially young ones. It was a "what will the market bear" analysis.

With this new financial focus, legal management consultants, including one that made a presentation to my firm, said law practice would follow the same consolidation trend as other business sectors and that, ultimately, there would be about twenty dominant firms in the country. When these firm consolidations occurred, the consultants said, the combined firms would shed or downsize less profitable practices (and lawyers) and focus on growing more lucrative ones or acquiring profitable practices from other firms by offering greater incomes and support to expand their practices. Splitting profits among more lawyers would require increased profits, putting pressure to raise rates. Premium billing would become an important profit-producing driver, necessitating marketing for cases and transactions that could sustain higher hourly rates.

As consolidations occurred, as projected, firms fixed their attention on increasing profits per partner. It worked. From 1985 to 2019, the average PPP increased at the largest one hundred firms from $325,500 to just shy of $2 million. Legal services began to look more like a profit-generating commodity, not a service profession. Profitability became the watchword for success.

This focus on firm profitability, financial performance, and escalating incomes took a toll as lawyers began working longer hours. The number of law firm partners on the boards of non-profits decreased significantly. Pro bono services became as much a tool to recruit law firm graduates as it did a public good. Associates worked longer hours. Associate salaries increased at the best firms as they fished in a shallow pool of the brightest young lawyers in an effort to staff premium billed cases.[2] As salaries at large firms increased, there was price pressure to increase salaries for associates at smaller firms as they tried to recruit their share of the best and brightest who declined the allure of large-firm practice. All of this required the generation of more revenue, which only exacerbated the cycle.

There was other evidence of this shift toward a profits-centric model of law practice. Firms began paying bonuses to associates and partners based on their work production, often heavily weighted by the number of hours billed in a year or the new business generated. As a result, busy, experienced partners had less time to mentor young lawyers as demand for production and revenue increased. Annual partner draws and associate compensation became increasingly tied to hours worked and fees billed, putting pressure on everyone to work more and spend more time searching for new business opportunities.

In more recent years, this obsession with business performance has become attractive to non-lawyer investors who want to participate in high-return legal outcomes. Today, certain funds offer returns to those willing to pool their money to invest in risky, but potentially lucrative, litigation. In a 2016 *Forbes* article, Daniel Fisher wrote about this trend, focusing on Mighty Group Inc., a company offering double-digit returns. How were these returns generated? Fisher explained: "Mighty lends money to plaintiffs in personal injury lawsuits. You collect only if they

---

[2] Lawyers right out of law school now make six-figure salaries at large law firms, unimaginable when I began practicing law.

do. Plus, the head of this online electronic investment platform recommends that only personal-injury lawyers, or investors who have such lawyers helping them evaluate cases, plunk down their money."[3] Mighty Group is not the only player in this litigation-financing market. Burford Capital has its own business model in financially supporting civil cases: "Burford provides capital to law firms on a single-case and portfolio basis, at every stage of the legal process, including fees and expenses. We act as passive investors and do not control strategy or settlement decision-making, and our capital is almost always provided as a non-recourse investment, shifting risk from the firm to Burford."[4] It explains its litigation-finance services in the "Litigation Finance 101" section of its website:

> With legal finance, a litigant or a law firm uses the asset value of commercial litigation or arbitration to secure capital from a third party, either to finance the litigation or for more general business purposes. In its most common form, legal finance is provided on a single-case basis to pay for costs associated with commercial litigation or arbitration (lawyers' fees, case expenses, etc.) in exchange for a portion of the ultimate award or settlement. Often, this approach fulfills the needs of companies that can't afford or don't want to pay their lawyers by the hour, or of law firms that wish to offer clients flexible terms but can't or don't want to assume the entire contingent risk of doing so. Increasingly, however, legal finance is used in ways resembling specialty corporate finance. Companies and law firms use legal finance to move cost and risk off balance sheets, free up capital for other business purposes and improve risk management while adding

---

[3] https://www.forbes.com/sites/danielfisher/2016/01/20/the-next-great-investment-idea-somebody-elses-lawsuit/#767e59125102

[4] https://www.burfordcapital.com/how-we-work/with-law-firms/

budgetary certainty. A particularly fast-growing area of legal finance is portfolio-based finance, where multiple matters (both plaintiff and defense matters) are combined in a single cross-collateralized financing arrangement.[5]

There are other telltale signs of the shift to law as business. Just drive down the road or watch TV, and you'll see firms advertising for new business. The other night I saw an ad in which a client said her lawyer got her the money she deserved "and more." New business is best generated, apparently, by touting that a lawyer can get you more than is just.

Has this pivot from profession to business been good for practitioners? Evidently not. According to an article in the *New York Times* on August 17, 1990, "Job dissatisfaction among lawyers is widespread, profound and growing worse."[6] How much worse could it get? Fast-forward almost thirty years, and let's look at the data.

The Unhealthy Effects of a Profit-First Profession

In 2017, *Mental Health Daily* observed, "It seems as though in the United States, jobs requiring significant levels of aptitude, sacrifice, and education seem to be those with above-average risk of suicide."[7] Among the careers in the top-ten list of suicide occurrences? Attorneys.

A few years ago, I made a continuing-legal-education presentation on professionalism. I followed a talk about a State Bar of Georgia initiative to address suicide among Georgia

---

[5] Ibid.

[6] http://www.nytimes.com/1990/08/17/us/law-at-the-bar-more-lawyers-are-less-happy-at-their-work-a-survey-finds.html

[7] https://mentalhealthdaily.com/2015/01/06/top-11-professions-with-highest-suicide-rates/

lawyers. Regrettably, the presenters reported that the bar's sui-
cide-prevention program was still going strong because of the
alarmingly high incidence of suicides associated with the profession.

Research shows that lawyers have the eleventh highest incidence of suicide among professions.[8] The issue of suicides
among lawyers is troubling. Still, a survey of the internet dis-
closes little information about the actual number of suicides
among lawyers in our country. Maybe that is because there is
insufficient data. Maybe it is because we don't want to know.
Still, most in the legal industry know that practicing law takes a
toll on mental health. In 2017, the then managing director of
the firm BCG Attorney Search wrote an article entitled "25 Reasons Most Attorneys Hate the Practice of Law and Go Crazy
(And What to Do about It)."[9] As of July 16, 2021, the article
had 207,102 views and 2,126 votes, averaging a 4.7 out of 5 approval rating for the article's content.

The American Bar Association established an initiative to
address mental health issues in law practice. Euphemistically
named the "Working Group to Advance Well-Being in the Legal Profession," the group recommends that firms sign a pledge
to address the disturbing increase in mental health and substance
abuse issues among practitioners. Specifically, the ABA is

> calling upon legal employers (including law firms, corpo-
> rate entities, government agencies and legal aid organi-
> zations) to first: (a) recognize that substance use and
> mental health problems represent a significant challenge
> for the legal profession and acknowledge that more can
> and should be done to improve the health and well-being

---

[8] https://www.abajournal.com/magazine/article/attorney_sui-
cide_what_every_lawyer_needs_to_know
[9] https://www.lawcrossing.com/article/900042544/25-Reasons-
Why-Most-Attorneys-Go-Crazy-And-What-to-Do-About-It/

of lawyers; and (b) pledge to support the Campaign and work to adopt and prioritize its seven-point framework for building a better future.[10]

More than 195 firms, corporations, and law schools have signed the pledge. The pledge requests a commitment to consider mental health and addiction programs. It does not include addressing the number of hours worked or their effect on mental health or attorney well-being. The online service Law360 reports on the "well-being" offerings at firms. These offerings range from confidential employee assistance, health-counseling contacts, meditation rooms, and even chair massages. How have those well-being initiatives worked? There are no reported changes to the mental health and substance abuse issues faced by modern firms, likely because the underlying demands and stresses of modern profit-driven law businesses remain unchanged. Note, however, that the impact of COVID-19 on suicide rates is being studied to determine if they rose during the pandemic. Maybe this will result in better data.

I have been involved in litigation and trial practice for more than forty years as a lawyer, a litigation manager, and federal judge. For forty years, I've watched the erosion of lawyer satisfaction. Meditation, massages, and better lawyer referral services are not going to course correct the profession, especially in the practice of civil litigation where, in my experience, dissatisfaction and distress among lawyers is most severe.[11]

---

[10] https://www.americanbar.org/groups/lawyer_assistance/well-being-in-the-legal-profession/

[11] In a 2011 law review article written by Jerome M. Organ and published in *The University of St. Thomas Law Journal*, Mr. Organ reviewed data and findings of lawyer satisfaction in articles published by various organizations (St. Thomas Law Journal, 8 [2011]: 225). He found that the level of lawyer dissatisfaction was exaggerated and stated the empirical data suggests lawyers are "somewhat satisfied,"

Don't Play the Lottery;
Practice the Profession

The law as a business-first—and for some, a business-only—career is a trend that drives job dissatisfaction for too many lawyers. It has changed how everything from big-law defense firms to small-shop plaintiff firms lawyers practice our profession. There is evidence of it in the most unlikely of places.

The changing face of law—from profession to business—was highlighted in the gym just days before I wrote this chapter. There in the weight room I overheard two lawyers talking about a case that had been tried by a plaintiff lawyer friend of theirs. The lawyer had won a $240-million verdict in a personal injury trial the week before. They both marveled at a verdict that large—maybe the largest ever awarded in the state. One of the attorneys said the punitive damages award might have to be reduced because of the state's $250,000 cap on punitive damages. Even with the reduction, the other commented, the lawyer's

---

"satisfied," or "highly satisfied" with their work at 70 to 80 percent levels. What Mr. Organ does not do is explain what "satisfaction" means. Does it mean fulfilled in serving others or does it mean adequately compensated for the burden of the work required? Even if defined as fulfilment or enthusiasm in lawyer's work, being just "satisfied" or "somewhat satisfied" is a poor reflection of the state of the profession. I think lawyers want more out of their professional endeavors. One thing he does note is that lawyers in practice for a greater number of years seem more "satisfied" in their work than those who have entered the profession more recently, and those in public service positions are generally "satisfied" at greater levels than those in private practice. That, I believe, is true, because experienced lawyers have had time to align their values with their work, and those who choose public service, with its concomitant lower salary levels (when compared to "big law"), show a lawyer's willingness to forgo compensation to do work that aligns with their values. More about alignment later.

legal fees would be a "pretty good payday." There was no mention of the impact on the plaintiff, no mention of whether the result was just or justifiable. The interest was in their friend's winning ticket in what they viewed as the litigation lottery.

The business-first approach to law has obscured our view of who we are. The practice of law is a noble profession, and being a lawyer is a solemn privilege. It is a calling to serve others, to seek justice and fair outcomes for our clients. The profession carries with it the duty to maintain the people's trust in the judicial system. Our callings and duties should shape what we do and who we are, not PPP.

The strong winds of the marketplace are disrupting our alignment with the historical callings, duties, and values of the legal profession. This book is about how to withstand these winds of change and offers some guidance on how to restore the honor of what we do. Ultimately, it is a book about returning to our core values and aligning our practices to them.

We are entrusted to serve those who seek our help. Sometimes financial rewards will come as a result, but material reward is not our endgame. If we continue to take this business-first approach, many of us will continue to spend our legal careers feeling lost, and our careers unfulfilling. Others will find themselves continuing to wander in the wilderness, desperate to find a path out. This book urges you to ask, Am I aligning how I practice with the professional and personal values that I hold true—those in which I believe? Let's examine how alignment can revive our practices and restore our profession.

Chapter 2

The Aligned Lawyer

"One of the great satisfactions in life is aligning your conduct to your value system."
—*Jon Ericson, speech communications professor and writer*

"What's money? A man is a success if he gets up in the morning and goes to bed at night and in between does what he wants to do."
—*Bob Dylan, songwriter and musician*

Years ago, I read a book by Stephen Carter entitled *Integrity*. Carter is a lawyer with scores of professional accomplishments. He graduated from Yale Law School and clerked for Justice Thurgood Marshall. He is a versatile and prolific writer, and his works include magazine articles, public policy papers, and nonfiction books. As if this were not enough, he's earned recognition from the *New York Times* as a best-selling fiction author. In his book, Carter defines "integrity" this way: "When I refer to integrity I have something very simple and very specific in mind. Integrity, as I will use the term, requires three steps: (1) *discerning* what is right and what is wrong; (2) *acting* on what you have discerned, even at personal cost; and (3) *saying openly* that you are acting on your understanding of right from wrong."[1] I've

---

[1] *Integrity*, 5–7.

often used Carter's integrity template to discuss how we practice law, and more importantly, how we live our lives. Carter's core teaching is that we must align our conduct with our values. In my estimation, what's missing in our legal culture today are attorneys who don't do the hard work to determine what they believe in, what they value. And how can you align your conduct to your values if you don't know what they are? Worse yet are those attorneys who have done the hard work to figure out their values, but then decline to align their conduct with them. For them, William Shakespeare said it best: "God hath given you one face and you make yourselves another."[2]

In the chase for advancement, status, or a greater share of the profit, many lawyers have failed to align their practice with their values or the values of the profession. This alignment failure is a fundamental reason too many lawyers are unsatisfied, unsettled, unhappy, or unfulfilled in their work. I believe it's a fundamental reason why addiction, mental health issues, and suicide plague the profession.

In the three stories I shared in the introduction to this book, each lawyer was misaligned and felt lost or trapped, or both. Take Stu, for instance. He hadn't defined the impact he wanted to have as a lawyer, so he didn't know the kind of law he should practice. His alignment failure affected his professional satisfaction and that, in turn, affected his relationships and his health. In my discussions with Stu, I found him to be a smart, practical fellow who valued contact with people. In his medium-sized firm, he did fine legal work but was denied direct client contact, something he craved and something he believed was important in serving a client. He was told client contact would come in time, but until then, he had to work hard for others who were tasked with serving clients more directly. His client-contactless existence meant long, unsatisfying hours. The only place he could unload his frustration was at home, on the one he cared

---

[2] Shakespeare, *Hamlet*, act 3, sc. 1.

for the most and the person least responsible for his job dissatis-faction. His wife's take? She understood his dilemma, and while she couldn't resolve it, she was willing to support a move to a position that he found more satisfying, even if it meant less money.

John's case was different. His misalignment developed over time as he grew dissatisfied with his day-to-day legal work, and he wanted work that had impact beyond the bottom line. His resolution was to respond to a public-service opportunity, where he believed his advice and counsel would matter to his commu-nity and his country. He was willing to move to a new city for a couple of years for a new work experience, but his family resisted because they appreciated the lifestyle his business-first practice provided. So, he stayed where he was. Even though he knew his values, he was unable to align his work to them because of his family's preferences. New work and his family were important priorities, but moving to a job in Washington at a reduced in-come prohibited him from balancing the priorities of his family. He didn't explore other moves where he might have aligned with both priorities. Alignment is never a one-and-only or a one-and-done proposition.

Joann was misaligned from the start. After discussing her possible job loss, I asked what kind of practice she wanted. She didn't know. So, I asked her a simple question: "Why did you go to law school?" She told me she enrolled because her dad con-vinced her that among her options, being a lawyer provided the most financial security. I asked what she would have done after college if she hadn't attended law school. In a moment her un-certainty vanished. She lit up when she told me how she loved her public relations coursework in college and how her intern-ship at a public relations firm had been a rich experience. She wondered whether she could use her public relations skills to help others, and whether it was too late to look for work in that field. I suggested she think about modifying her course and said there was plenty of public relations work in the legal profession, including helping lawyers explain their practices and experience, letting the public know about a firm's outreach into the community, and helping design presentations to prospective clients about a firm's competencies. This was something she hadn't considered. She had not allowed her interests to drive her desire to serve others. As a result, she aligned herself to someone else's values—in this case, her father—and was slogging it out doing dissatisfying work.[3]

Begin with Alignment

Aligning your conduct with your values—living with integrity— is key to finding fulfilling and meaningful work in the practice of law. But increasingly, it is overlooked as we opt instead to evaluate law-practice success according to business standards. Sure, there are aligned lawyers. I know lawyers who understood that the practice of law is fundamentally about serving clients, whether by structuring a transaction or helping in a dispute, and in doing so love what they do. They see the value of this service to others apart from the monetary awards. Others I know observed the tension and hard work required of a trial and thought they would do well in that environment. They understand that trials serve as a means of achieving justice, of righting wrongs in a commercial transaction, or holding people accountable who committed crimes. Others thrive building a firm to identify and meet the legal needs of people and companies. These individuals are often good lawyers, but better organizational leaders. People who fundamentally value client service and who seek just results in disputes and fair commercial agreements enter law to advance those values and are often aligned from the start.

---

[3] As of the writing of this book, Joann has had a couple of leads in the public relations field, including making the short list for a position. More about Joann, and the rest of her story, later.

Others were attracted to the practice of law because of the esteem of the legal profession. For them, entry into it is itself an accomplishment. They may have had a sense of the type of practice they'd find rewarding but followed a less direct path to finding a job where they'd thrive. They found alignment because they had the courage to move one or more times before they landed where they were fulfilled. Others were forced to move because they failed where they were, sometimes because of misalignment, but their failure forced them to work hard to find satisfying, aligned work.

There are others, though, who were exposed to the tensions of legal work and who concluded they valued other things more—time with family, community service, or other career opportunities—and determined that law practice was, therefore, not for them. And their decision not to practice law was also an alignment decision. Part of determining alignment is discovering what you value and whether practicing law can integrate with it.

Aligning Your Conduct to Your Values Is an Ongoing Process

Finding alignment requires a willingness to undertake the critical self-evaluation necessary to determine where you are and where you want to go. This process often is aided by wise counsel from those who've aligned their practices to their values.

Anthony clerked for me when I was on the bench. He has an interesting background, which included service as an officer in the Marine Corps. He loved leading and managing Marines and thought he might enjoy the practice of law in the military. He went to law school through a funded legal-education program, graduated from a respected law school with honors, and served as an officer in the Judge Advocate General's Corps before leaving active duty.

Anthony became a law clerk in our chambers, hoping to transition to private practice—a smart, practical decision. His wife, whom he adores, had an arrangement with her employer in Washington, DC, to work from home in Atlanta and travel back to DC when needed. He has two delightful daughters and is a committed dad. Immediately upon moving to Atlanta, he found a good neighborhood, rented a house, and worked to assimilate into his new community.

As a clerk, Anthony worked hard and with undistracted focus. He listened well and was well-liked by everyone. He served in the reserves while he clerked and scheduled his reserve duties on weekend days so they would not interfere with his work for the court. He had strong values. He oriented his life to them. The alignment of his conduct to his values was obvious.

As Anthony neared the end of his clerkship, we talked about his next steps. He was focused on an opportunity in Washington, DC, with an agency involved in national-security issues. He was interested in the work, but it did not strike me as a good fit for him, nor was it consistent with his ambitions for his family, and I told him so. I didn't think the agency would give him credit or compensation for the value of his military service, something he was entitled to. I also didn't think he'd be given the autonomy he deserved and would end up stuck in a bureaucracy that would be a barrier to any contribution he could make. If adequate recognition wasn't given him and he had to suffer the glacial movement of a government office, I didn't think he'd enjoy the work environment.

We continued to talk about his career over the course of a few weeks, and like every bright, driven, head-strong young lawyer, he stubbornly focused on the Washington opportunity. I encouraged him, probably more than he wanted, to cast a wider net, if for no other reason than to get a better indication of his marketability. He did (maybe to appease me), and as he did, he more actively evaluated his values and what was important to him and his family. His wife, family, and the community he'd built in Atlanta were important.

Anthony warmed to the idea of deepening his roots in Atlanta and considered options for private practice. He was drawn to employment law, his interest in the practice area having been piqued during his clerkship. He applied to firms that had an employment-law focus and remained adamant about finding a firm that would allow him to work unconventional hours to free up time for his family.

I knew Anthony's preferred hours well. He liked to begin work before dawn, a start time he'd grown accustomed to when on active duty. He also wanted to leave slightly earlier than other lawyers. His preferred schedule resulted in him working eleven-hour days, but leaving in the early evening gave him more time with his girls. It wasn't just family time that Anthony valued. He also wanted collegiality in his practice and a firm that avoided polarizing internal politics. These values drew him to look for a position in smaller firms.

An Atlanta employment-law practice with about two dozen lawyers hired him. They were a group of driven lawyers who worked hard, but they were committed to collegiality and civility in their practice. They were open to his adjusted work schedule. They valued his previous leadership experience and committed to utilizing his talents. It was a terrific fit.

Because Anthony's values were aligned with his firm's, he excelled in and enjoyed his practice. A few years later, his values refined further. He found he wanted to travel less, have greater continuity in his representation of clients, and be more involved in his community. So, when he was asked to join the small employment-law division of a major Atlanta company, he made a move. Another perfect fit. The other day I learned he is moving to a new company where his values are even a better fit with his work.

Anthony's career choices are evidence of a man who aligned his career with his values from beginning to end. For years, his values were perfectly aligned with the mission of the Marine Corps. There, he saw the value active-duty lawyers offered to their units, and he applied for the funded legal-education program which allowed him to serve as a JAG Corps lawyer aligned to the mission of his unit. After his military stint was over, and wanting more opportunity to observe trials, he become a trial judge's clerk. Valuing his family, community, and a collegial atmosphere, he sought a job at a private law firm whose values aligned with his. And, even though successful in private practice, he moved to an in-house position for greater client continuity and flexibility to tend to his family and the community where he lived. And when he found an in-house position that provided even better alignment, he moved there.

As far as I know, Anthony never made a business-first, money-first decision. He's allowed his values to direct his career. For as long as I've known him, he's remained well-aligned in a job that provides compensation that is generous, and he is fulfilled in his work.

Alignment Begins with Personal Values

Alignment begins by determining your values, just like Anthony did. There are two basic types. Personal values are overarching and govern one's life. These should take into account your spouse and children. They may include some spiritual component or commitment to a particular worldview, or both. Personal values can include a commitment to public service and the community. Creative processes, teamwork and collaboration, work autonomy—these can also be values that are personal.

In practice, these values may move a lawyer to organize their work-life balance to maximize engagement with school-age children in their activities, or inspire someone to commit a percentage of their time to support a charity or their church.

Someone aligned to their core values may look for a work setting where they have flexibility to give more time at home or for community service, even if a position in that environment commands a lower salary. Someone who values philanthropy might choose to work long hours to make more money so they can have greater philanthropic impact, even if that requires unconventional hours to allow time with family and friends. A lawyer's overarching personal values should inform every decision. They are the background colors on the canvas on which the portrait of one's life and career is painted.

Professional values are the second value set to which practice must align. In the case of lawyers, these are the shared values of our profession. They are the more specific strokes that paint the portrait of every legal career. Different firms, business entities, and public agencies or departments might emphasize different professional focuses, but to practice within them, lawyers still must align their values to the environment they choose. For example, if you enjoy business, you may want to seek to practice in a firm that litigates commercial disputes where, if you value honesty, you are expected to demand honesty in the clients you represent. If you choose to work in an employment-law practice that innately values fairness in the workplace, you'll need to practice in a firm that values civility with lawyers and parties you oppose. If you elect to represent the government or defendants in criminal cases, you'll want to choose a firm that believes in requiring candor with their client and the court. If ethical conduct in dealing with others is a core value for you, you might want to look for a position on a legal staff committed to the company's compliance with regulatory demands. If you value protecting the rights of others, you may want to serve as counsel to a law enforcement agency committed to ensuring officers know and comply with the legal requirements for valid searches and seizures. Only when these two sets of values are determined—the personal and professional values you hold—can a lawyer find a practice with which to align.

A lawyer I've met recently named Seth proves that this alignment process works even where values are untraditional. Seth is bright and conscientious, but his values are different. On the background of his portrait are colors representing his interest in creative processes, especially writing. His family is central to what he values. He values practicing law in a collegial environment. His faith is central to his life. He wants to work in a place where he can write and practice law and apply his passion for writing to the legal work performed by his partners. And for that he searched hard.

Seth found a medium-sized firm that allowed him to write creatively and practice traditionally. His writing interest was new to the firm, but they took the risk to allow it. It is a firm that values collegiality and is open-minded about new ideas. What Seth and his firm did not know was that Seth's interest and skill as a writer would provide real value to those in the firm trying to communicate more effectively and creatively in legal briefs and reports to clients. His alignment is unusual, and his creative skill is viewed as a key asset to his colleagues, advances the work of the firm, satisfies Seth's drive to be a productive member of his practice, and is, to boot, profitable for his firm and for him.

I have my own story of having to make personal value choices in my legal career. King & Spalding is a large, successful law firm in Atlanta at which I was privileged to be a partner. In the late 1990s, an opportunity and a challenge came up which affected the hours I had available to work. The first was personal and involved a member of my family with unexpected health issues. I wanted and needed time to help him navigate his treatment. The second was an invitation to join a Leadership Atlanta class. The class invitation was rare, and the program lasted a year. Sessions occurred during work hours and in the evenings. By participating, I knew I'd learn more about my city, its programs, problems, and vision. I wanted to attend but questioned if I could help my family member and be in a Leadership Atlanta class.

Helping a family member and joining Leadership Atlanta were important to me and reflected two of my important personal core values—being available to my family and engaging my community. But both would affect my availability to work cases and market for new matters, thereby potentially affecting my overall compensation in the coming year due to the subsequent effect on the firm's profitability. I concluded that if it did, helping my family and getting a greater understanding of my community was reward enough. I'd found alignment requires awareness and commitment to personal values and then acting in ways consistent with them. It is the courage to act on the conviction of what you believe, something Carter said in his integrity definition.

Even though big law, as we call it, is often considered the cauldron that brews lawyer dissatisfaction, that isn't always fair. There are plenty of aligned lawyers in large national and international law firms who are fulfilled by their work. I know highly aligned lawyers at large firms who find immense satisfaction wrestling with hard legal issues and serving clients in the most difficult cases and transactions. They are paid well because they delve deep into seemingly impossible problems and can master how the law applies to them. If you sit with them over a beer, they will regale you with the challenges of finding the right answer to a client's problem and the challenges of trial work or seeking fair resolutions. It is unlikely they ever will talk about the fees they generate, the compensation they receive, or the houses that they own. Their love is the law. If you talk with their families, they will tell you the same. Their children may complain they wished their parent did not work so hard, but they almost always conclude by saying that their mom or dad love what they do, and they want the same in life—to be fulfilled by their work.

Frank Jones was a prominent big-firm Atlanta lawyer. A lawyer's lawyer, clients hired him to represent them in their most important cases. He was a master advocate, including in the arguments he made before the United States Supreme Court. Yet he always had time to counsel, and correct, lawyers who worked with him. Money was never his driving force. Practicing law was. That was clear to me when, one day, while still at the peak of his career, he announced with another senior partner they were both reducing the amount of money they were entitled to receive each year. Why? Because they wanted more money to be available so more young lawyers could be elected partners of the firm.

The Intrigue of Seeking Alignment

My values were defined early in my career. I believed the legal system was designed to seek justice for people and that it was a lawyer's duty to achieve it. I also believed in serving others, and that was more important than money. And I believed in fairness and abiding by the rules. I thought the law did not work unless the playing field was level for everyone, whatever their circumstances or characteristics. I thought litigation lawyers should play fair but were also entitled to play hard. And, as it would turn out, these core values wouldn't change much over the years.

I started my career as a member of the Air Force Judge Advocate General's Corps, where my job each day was to protect the interests of the government and to ensure the government was fair in its dealings with people and complied with the law which governed its conduct. In the latter part of my air force active duty, I prosecuted service members who were alleged to have committed felony offenses. In these duties I held those accountable who committed crimes, and, as a result, I helped make the community safer. Each of these duties aligned with my personal and professional values, and the professional values of the places that employed me.

I left the air force because as JAG officers rose in rank, they were moved into management positions, and did less legal work. I wanted to be a practicing lawyer, so I moved to private practice and joined a firm where I could litigate cases with different subject matters. I thrived on the complexity of the work and the sophistication of the legal issues because I valued difficult assignments and hard work. As the years wore on, however, I found I was unsettled by what I was doing.

I had a number of discussions with confidants who helped me identify why I'd become dissatisfied in my practice. One morning, as I met with one of them, I had sort of an epiphany. I discovered that I loved my work in the air force because it was value oriented. Each day I was called to do the right, fair thing. In private practice, I loved the challenge of the work and the complexity of the issues, but the results were more often about money than justice. My practice was just too oriented toward the material. So, I began the process of realigning my career with my personal and professional values, and a couple of years later I reentered public service. I spent the next seventeen years in the Department of Justice and federal judiciary. I found these jobs provided complex and challenging work that made a difference in people's lives and my community. I was energized by my responsibility to make sure the playing field was level for all litigants and in helping them to conclude disputes. I was dead serious about ensuring fairness in criminal trials—a value especially important to me. And because my values aligned with the values of the job, I found the work abundantly satisfying.

I've taken alignment analysis seriously over the years. It has been critical for me, and it is critical for every lawyer whether they just passed the bar exam or they're far along in their career. At every stage of our legal career, we must discern what we value and whether what we are doing aligns with what we deem important. And if we don't know what we value, we need to take the time to find out what that is. That often begins with asking ourselves why we went to law school and what motivated us then to endure the pressures we faced in our studies. It also requires us to think hard about what is important in life, which work we enjoy, what we don't, and whether what we are accomplishing really makes a difference.

When is the last time you considered your personal and professional values? When was the last time you reviewed the values that are innate to your profession, your practice area, or your place of employment? And when was the last time you took an inventory of the personal values that are important to you and asked whether you've compromised them to get ahead? Have you forgotten the oaths that should inform your professional values? That's a critical question, so let's pause here and remember the oaths you took and the promises you made before you were given the privilege of practicing law.

Chapter 3

The Shared Values of the Profession

"There are others for whom planning comes hard. They put off every detail until the last minute and move through life in a kind of breathless confusion. They depend upon chance and the particular circumstance to determine what must or must not be done."
—*Howard Thurmond*, The Inward Journey

On the walls of my office hang each of the commissions authorizing me to serve in the various public offices to which I was appointed. These include my commission as an air force officer, as the United States Attorney in my district, as deputy independent counsel, and, finally, as a United States district judge. After each of these appointments I was permitted to begin my duties only after taking an oath.

An oath is a somber and solemn promise often taken before God to uphold certain principles or values.[1] My oaths were all taken in public, and each time I placed my hand on my Bible and promised to do my duty to serve the office faithfully.

Of particular importance to me is the oath I took before assuming my duties on the bench as a federal judge. I stood before federal and state judges, members of the state bar, law

---

[1] *Webster's Dictionary* defines it as: "a solemn usually formal calling upon God or a god...to witness that one sincerely intends to do what one says." https://www.merriam-webster.com/dictionary/oath

THE SHARED VALUES OF THE PROFESSION

enforcement officials, federal prosecutors and defense lawyers, state and federal dignitaries, my closest and dearest friends, and my wife and my sons. I raised my right hand and said, "I, William S. Duffey Jr., do solemnly swear or affirm that I will administer justice without respect to persons, and do equal right to the poor and to the rich, and that I will faithfully and impartially discharge and perform all the duties incumbent upon me as a federal district judge, under the Constitution, agreeably to the constitution and laws of the United States. So help me God." In the presence of public witnesses, I made my promise to uphold the values of my office. And every federal judge makes the same promise I made that day. We are bound by the same values.

It's not just judges who take oaths. Every member of our profession admitted to practice takes an oath to uphold the duties incumbent on being an officer of the court. You probably remember that day. It was likely a public proceeding attended by other lawyers, colleagues, court officials, friends, and family. The ceremony was memorable. But my suspicion is that few lawyers remember the details of the proceeding other than that they were "sworn in" at the ceremony. I'll bet they don't remember the specific words in the oath they took, or the values they promised to uphold in their practices.

The Shared Values We Promised to Practice

I was admitted as a lawyer in South Carolina, the state where I first took an oath to uphold certain values in the practice of law. I took that oath a long time ago, and I can't recall the exact wording used in 1977. But I know the oath South Carolina lawyers take today, and it is clear and serious. It's a bit more detailed than the oath I took, but the promises were much the same. Here is the oath used now:

Lawyer's Oath

I do solemnly swear (or affirm) that:

I am duly qualified, according to the Constitution of this State, to exercise the duties of the office to which I have been appointed, and that I will, to the best of my ability, discharge those duties and will preserve, protect and defend the Constitution of this State and of the United States;

I will maintain the respect and courtesy due to courts of justice, judicial officers, and those who assist them;

To my clients, I pledge faithfulness, competence, diligence, good judgment and prompt communication;

To opposing parties and their counsel, I pledge fairness, integrity, and civility, not only in court, but also in all written and oral communications;

I will not pursue or maintain any suit or proceeding which appears to me to be unjust nor maintain any defenses except those I believe to be honestly debatable under the law of the land, but this obligation shall not prevent me from defending a person charged with a crime;

I will employ for the purpose of maintaining the causes confided to me only such means as are consistent with trust and honor and the principles of professionalism, and will never seek to mislead an opposing party, the judge or jury by a false statement of fact or law;

I will respect and preserve inviolate the confidences of my clients, and will accept no compensation in connection with a client's business except from the client or with the client's knowledge and approval;

I will maintain the dignity of the legal system and advance no fact prejudicial to the honor or reputation of a party or witness, unless required by the justice of the cause with which I am charged;

I will assist the defenseless or oppressed by ensuring that justice is available to all citizens and will not delay any person's cause for profit or malice;

[So help me God.]

The Lawyer's Oath—in whatever form administered—serves as an acknowledgement that we are governed by principles we share.[2] It is the doorway through which we enter the practice

---

[2] The chief justice of the Supreme Court of Georgia in 1989 created the Chief Justice's Commission on Professionalism, which developed the Lawyer's Creed and Aspirational Statement on Professionalism. In 1990, these were incorporated into the Rules and Regulations for the Organization and Government of the State Bar of Georgia, of which I am now a member. The Creed and Aspirational Statement was enacted based on a concern about the erosion of professional standards in Georgia. The Lawyer's Creed, like the South Carolina oath, is comprehensive and specific:

A LAWYER'S CREED

To my clients, I offer faithfulness, competence, diligence, and good judgment. I will strive to represent you as I would want to be represented and to be worthy of your trust.

To the opposing parties and their counsel, I offer fairness, integrity, and civility. I will seek reconciliation and, if we fail, I will strive to make our dispute a dignified one.

To the courts, and other tribunals, and to those who assist them, I offer respect, candor, and courtesy. I will strive to do honor to the search for justice.

To my colleagues in the practice of law, I offer concern for your welfare. I will strive to make our association a professional friendship.

of law. It reminds us that practicing law is not a job, but rather an appointment to a public office and the admission to a noble profession. Our first duty is not to profits-per-partner, but to the people we serve and the institution of the judiciary. It is a profession that requires trust, honor, dignity, fairness, and integrity. These are our shared values, the foundation of our conduct, and our service to others. These are the values to which our practices must align.

The Tyranny of Expectations

Alignment is not always easy, even to those shared values that are supposed to govern the practice of law. There are often barriers that prevent it, or at least make it harder. These pressures are subtle but powerful. They come from unexpected places. Most are rooted in what I call the "tyranny of the expectation of others," a concept I learned about firsthand when I was in undergraduate school.

To the profession, I offer assistance. I will strive to keep our business a profession and our profession a calling in the spirit of public service.

To the public and our systems of justice, I offer service. I will strive to improve the law and our legal system, to make the law and our legal system available to all, and to seek the common good through the representation of my clients.

The Aspirational Statement is too long to restate verbatim, but the reasons it was passed are insightful. Here they are: "The Court believes there are unfortunate trends of commercialization and loss of professional community in the current practice of law. These trends are manifested in an undue emphasis on the financial rewards of practice, a lack of courtesy and civility among members of our profession, a lack of respect for the judiciary and for our systems of justice, and a lack of regard for others and for the common good. As a community of professionals, we should strive to make the internal rewards of service, craft, and character, and not the external reward of financial gain, the primary rewards of the practice of law."

Dr. Jon Ericson taught my undergraduate class on Speech and Human Behavior. There, we learned about the impact of values and social environment on our speech and our conduct. He was a multiyear recipient of the award for best undergraduate professor because he was an exceptional, insightful communicator and thinker. During one of his lectures, he offered this quote by the psychiatrist and philosopher Carl Jung: "The world will ask you who you are, and if you do not know, the world will tell you."

I might have been too young then to understand the quote fully, but with some life behind me, I discovered that what Jung said is true. Unless we determine who we are, and want to be, we will be defined by external forces. For lawyers, these forces might be the desire for more influence, power, or status. They may be internal pressures or pressures asserted by your colleagues and partners or your family. They might be powerful enough to cause a lawyer to succeed, to win at all cost. But in the long run, these sorts of pressures impede alignment, both with your personal and professional values and with the values you swore to uphold.

Recall Joann, the woman who became a lawyer because her father said it would be a good job. Her story is not uncommon; in fact, I've heard a similar one scores of times. And if I interviewed these parents who pushed their children toward law school, they'd likely say the same thing: *I encouraged my daughter to attend law school because I wanted her to have a viable, secure profession.* I suspect their parental direction was also calculated to make them look good in the eyes of their contemporaries. I understand both motivations. I am also a parent. In raising two now grown sons, I know the anxiety of releasing them to live their own lives, and I know how easy it is to view their successes and failures as my own.

I admit it. I had lots of internal deliberations about releasing my older son to attend college in Nashville. He wanted to become a bluegrass musician, and, in my mind, music was not a secure career track. I went so far as to research if he could double major in music business and music performance so he'd have a "practical" fallback. My wife wisely suggested that his life was not mine to live. Thank goodness for her intervention. I stopped foisting my expectations on Charles, and he made his own choices in college, eventually moving from the bluegrass performance curriculum to an accounting program. Today, he is the chief operating officer of a university medical practice. His bluegrass avocation is still strong. Giving Charles the freedom to make his own career choices allowed him to align his professional life according to his values, including the value of musical creativity. He loves what he does professionally and musically.

In the end, all we really want for our children is for them to be fulfilled in life. But parents can be a strong force in empowering alignment or impeding it by saddling their children with expectations. It's not just parents who do this. Law schools do too.

As a judge, I received many letters from law schools noting their strong law students and sharing how they would make fine law clerks. They offered to help me identify potential clerks and to facilitate the submission of their applications. It was not lost on me that these were form letters that had been mass mailed to federal judges across the country. How did I know? Because I did not hire recent graduates, and these law schools knew as much, or could have, with a search of the law-clerk-hiring website. I opted to hire clerks who had a few years of practice experience, no matter how good a potential law school graduate was. When I received these law school letters, I often looked at the school's websites and noted how often they touted the number of graduates who were hired as judicial clerks, information they made available to future law school applicants. I wondered if they carefully evaluated if their grads who became law clerks were aligned with federal clerkship work. I doubted it. If they didn't, I'd do my best to get this message of alignment out.

For example, I once was invited to speak to students at a prominent law school to discuss federal clerkships and the work clerks performed. I opened my comments by saying that many law graduates, even the top students in a class, should think hard about whether or not they should clerk. I told them that, depending on their practice preferences, they may benefit by entering practice immediately rather than joining a federal judge for one or two years right after law school. If they were interested in transactional work, for example, clerking would not necessarily help them develop the skills they needed and might not measurably increase their marketability. And for those interested, I told them each clerkship experience was different, and that firm-hiring committees knew which clerkships provided the most valuable training and experience. That is, not all clerkships were equally valuable. Why take one that didn't offer valuable experience or serve as a résumé enhancer? Why allow a school to direct you to a position that was not aligned with your personal and professional values?

Law schools that advertise how many students go on to clerk for federal judges also tend to advertise how many students are hired by large firms in major cities, often called "big law." These schools urge their most competitive students to apply to big law, too often without regard to whether those students' values are aligned with big-law practice. Why? Because these jobs pay the highest salaries and are perceived as commanding the most respect and providing the most important work. These prospects are enticing for students and their parents. In other words, law schools can highlight certain external considerations—big salaries, for instance—that draw students to apply.

For many graduates, though, big-law practices are not aligned with their personal and professional values. Sure, the experiences can offer excellent training and financial enrichment, but a big-law experience is demanding, and many new lawyers find it unsatisfying. If a young attorney isn't careful, the expectations of these firms can co-opt their values and delay their search for a practice in which they fit. For others, big law is a place to begin, but not necessarily to end. But it takes courage to set a course, follow it for a while, but limit the big-law experience to enough years to learn to write and research well, master other practice tools, and make some money to pay off student debt. Then it may be time to find alignment with your practice.

I worked in a major law firm for twenty years, and I acknowledge it presents challenging, highly compensated work. But I joined after my four-year experience as a military lawyer in which I tried a number of hard, important criminal cases to verdict. I knew how to try a case and thrived in work that was demanding. I was successful at it, and I was fulfilled doing it. I was, in short, aligned to it. So, knowing I wanted to expand my litigation experience in private practice, I joined King & Spalding. Because of my experience, I got into the courtroom earlier than my contemporaries and was the first of my group to try a case as first chair. In fact, I tried it alone. (And to be completely honest, I wasn't sure that was an especially good idea, even though the result was successful for our client.)

I enjoyed litigation practice in big law, but my personal and professional values were aligned to it from the start. I wasn't pressured into it by my dad or a law school. The allure of more money didn't motivate me. And if the big-law practice had asked me to violate the oaths I'd sworn as an attorney, I'd have left it all behind in a second. For me, big law was an invaluable training ground, as it is for others, but only if there is alignment between that kind of practice and the lawyer's values, even if only for a season.

No matter the job opportunity presented, each lawyer should consider how it aligns with their values and the values embedded within the oaths they took upon entering the profession. We won't always get it right. We won't be completely aligned with some jobs, but those serve as preparation for careers with which we will. So, throughout the course of your career, spot-check your alignment, and if you find yourself unaligned, explore other options.

The Death Knell of Alignment

Alignment is most significantly impeded by external forces, and our current culture of commercialism is perhaps the most prevalent. But there are other subtle influences that also draw us out of alignment. I admit there are some that influenced me.

I made partner at my firm in 1987. Betsy, my wife of now forty-three years, and from the beginning the love of my life, is a splendid mother and Clemson grad. In the late 1980s, she was embarking on her career as a children's book writer. When I made partner, Betsy and I committed to live in line with my associate-level income. We didn't begin looking at new houses or new cars, at least not at first. Months into my new status as partner, I realized the only thing that had changed was that I was making more money. And with that realization, I decided my new status should make some difference in my day-to-day life. So, I bought a BMW 528e, standard-shift sedan—a partner kind of car. A couple of years later, we decided to upgrade our house. Did I need a new car or home? Not really. But cars and houses are the objective, visible indicia of success to others, and I fell victim to their allure. Status and money pulled me out of alignment.

Although I didn't recognize it at the time, practice was becoming for me, a business. And the business-first ethos induced me to go out to find more legal work, for which I felt entitled to greater compensation. My appetite grew. I began wanting to eat what I killed.

The seduction—the allure of money and the acquisition of things—was coupled with my drive to compete. How was I doing when compared to others? I tried to resist this comparison trap, but I failed. The temptation to live by comparison to others confronted me in different ways. Our partnership was very democratic, and we shared a lot of financial information internally. Among the most personal was the final result of what was called our "accountability process," which involved the collection of quantitative and qualitative information about the contribution of each equity partner. Data was collected about hours worked, the amount billed (both individually and by others on matters opened by the responsible partner), the generation of new business, other work that contributed to the financial and reputational success of the firm, and the personal evaluation of other partners. The system was robust, quantifiable, and fair. These evaluations were used to determine the number of points each partner was allocated for the next three-year period. Point levels, in turn, determined the amount of annual income a partner could expect.

At the end of the accountability process, a typed list was distributed to each equity partner. Each partner's name was on the list and next to it was the number of points allocated to them. Partners appeared on the list from most to least points. The list was hand-delivered to each partner in a red number-ten business envelope.

One year, I could feel myself being drawn out of alignment by my fixation on money and stature. So, as a sort of spiritual discipline, I decided to resist comparing the points awarded to me with the points awarded to others. I planned to do so by looking only at the points allocated to me to determine if I thought they fairly represented my contribution over the previous three years. I folded the list so the only line I could see was the one with my name and my points. I looked at them, thought about my work, and believed the points allocated fairly represented my contribution. The level of compensation for all equity partners was, after all, significant and would increase over the upcoming years as profits increased. My evaluation of what was fair was based only on the money I'd receive. During the process, I did not think about how fulfilled I was, whether the demand on my time adversely affected my relationship with my family, or any criteria other than money. My sole focus was on what I was getting paid, knowing, tangentially, that it was greater than partners at other large firms in town. Having completed my "look at only my line" analysis, I put the point sheet back into its envelope, placed the envelope in my top desk drawer, and went back to work.

I wish I could say I resisted the temptation to compare myself to other attorneys, but I couldn't. A few days later I took the point sheet out of my drawer and looked at the entire list to see how I did in relation to others. I was drawn into what I pledged to avoid—a comparison with my partners. In making my comparison, I found dissatisfaction that others, who in my mind contributed less, received a greater number of points.

Christmas Card Comparisons

This is what lawyers do a lot—evaluate their success by comparing theirs with the success of others. They go to parties and evaluate the size and value of the home where another lawyer lives. They take note of who belongs to what country club. The lavish weddings of the children of lawyers serve as a measure of success. Even Christmas cards are used to prove success.

A couple of years in a row, I received a Christmas card from one lawyer that showed him standing in front of his Learjet. Another sent me a card each year of him at some exotic vacation destination. Other cards were expensive, artsy cards on which the lawyer and his family members' names were preprinted inside in gold-foil letters. Envelopes were often addressed by their assistants or had a preprinted address label.

On the other hand, I occasionally received cards from lawyers with either a handwritten note or a printed report on their family's activities over the past year. These cards were warm, often expressing gratitude for the work they did, for the support of their family, for the accomplishments of their kids, and for the friendship we shared. Thinking back, almost all of these notes came from lawyers who had well thought-out values and alignment in their work and life.

The aligned lawyer understands these values, professional and personal, and conforms their life to them. They resist living a life of comparison and are not tyrannized by the expectations of others. They work hard at staying aligned.

There are those who stay true to who they are. They continually engage in their own kind of alignment analysis, sometimes modifying their practices if needed. So, what do these kinds of aligned lawyers look like? Let me introduce you to a few.

Chapter 4

Aligned Lawyers: What Do They Look Like?

"There is no knowledge so hard to acquire as the
knowledge of how to live this life well and naturally."
—*Michel de Montaigne, French philosopher*

"A good book is not in the draft. It is in the rewrite."
—*Betsy Duffey, author (and my wife)*

My father was a Medical Service Corps officer who retired from
the navy after thirty-one years of active-duty service. After retirement, he became the administrator at a regional hospital in
rural South Carolina. When he took his private-sector job, I was
in my first year of law school at the University of South Carolina.

The summer after my second year, my father called me. He
was being fired by the hospital, he said, because of a decision
he'd made about a patient's room assignment. Although my dad
did not personally assign patient rooms, a member of the hospital board had called him to complain about the room assigned to
a member of his family. The board member explained that his
relative had been placed in a semi-private room, and he wanted
her to be placed in a private one.

My dad listened to the request, then told the board member
that the hospital had more admitted patients than it had rooms,
so a private-room assignment wasn't possible. The board member persisted and told my dad in no uncertain terms that his relative had to be moved because she objected to being in the same

room as a black patient. If the request wasn't accommodated, the board member warned, there would be consequences.

My dad refused to make the room change, he told me, because to do so was wrong. The hospital would not discriminate. The family member remained in her assigned room, and the next day the board fired my father.

My dad called, distraught and wondering whether he had any legal recourse for his discharge. I didn't know, I said, but I'd help him find a good attorney to advise him. After a little digging, I found a well-respected, well-trusted attorney with a strong reputation in employment cases. Within days of my father's termination, we were sitting in his office.

The attorney listened to the facts and reviewed some documents my dad brought with him. He discussed possible claims, the cost of litigation, and the prospects for success in trying the case. He forecasted practical considerations, such as the toll that airing this dispute publicly would take on him and my mother, and it was this practical impact that carried a lot of weight with my father. As he considered the counsel, he decided the burden on the family and my mother was too great, and he decided not to file a case against the hospital and the board.

My father ultimately took an administrator's position at a medical facility in another city in South Carolina. It wasn't much salve for the sting of being fired. Still, few sons get a front-row seat to their dad's dismissal because he chose to stand up for what is right. My dad's willingness to stay true to his beliefs became a foundational value in my practice of law.

The lawyer's advice had an affect on me, too. I watched an aligned lawyer advise my dad on the practical and legal impact of filing a lawsuit. The advice was honest and realistic. It allowed my dad to make a decision that aligned with his values as a husband. The impact on those he cared for the most was not worth his desire to right the wrong he suffered, and for that reason he didn't file suit. It was a powerful lesson about maintaining integrity in the practice of law and considering compassion, and those values are ones to which I adhered.

Throughout my career, I learned to align my practice to my values by studying others—both those who were aligned and those who were not. The lawyer who counseled my dad was my earliest example of an aligned lawyer, but the most compelling example was a lawyer with whom I had a decades-long professional and personal relationship. He was the person who offered the clearest example of what alignment looks like, even in a big-law context.

I first met Griffin B. Bell and his wife, Mary, at the King & Spalding Christmas party when I joined the firm in December 1981. He and Mrs. Bell came up to my wife, Betsy, and me when we arrived at the party. He said he had heard we were attending the event but joked how he wasn't sure if he'd recognize me in the sea of tuxedos and evening gowns. He said the firm declined to make people wear name tags because it would be an admission that everyone didn't know each other, even though the truth was that there were too many of us to know everyone else. I had met him only for a few minutes when I interviewed at the firm months earlier, so I was surprised to find out that he knew I was married to Betsy, had an infant son, had just left active duty with the air force, and had yet to take the Georgia bar exam. Most of the other attorneys we met had no idea who I was, but Judge Bell, one of the firm's most senior and prominent lawyers, had done his research well before we arrived.

Judge Bell had a distinguished career. He'd been at King & Spalding from 1953 to 1961, then served on the United States Court of Appeals in the Fifth Circuit from 1961 to 1976, served as the attorney general of the United States in the Carter administration until 1979, then returned to private practice at King & Spalding. I met Judge Bell (the only name I ever called him) in his second stint at King & Spalding. We would go on to work together for twenty-five years.

Judge Bell was an extraordinary lawyer. Even more, he was an exceptional teacher, citizen, and person. He handled some of the highest profile matters in the United States and abroad. He conducted the internal investigation of the financial firm EF Hutton after it pled guilty to mail and wire fraud. He led a small team to South Africa to evaluate the prospects for ending apartheid under the government in power. He was a lawyer's lawyer and was asked by many attorneys to give second opinions on matters because he was considered a straight shooter, had unparalleled practical intellect and wisdom, and because lawyers trusted that he would not poach their clients. He was folksy and straight talking. He cared a lot about the legal profession.

In my early years, Judge Bell represented Clemson University regarding the tax implications of Senator Strom Thurmond's decision to contribute his personal papers to Clemson. I worked on the case with a small team of lawyers. By the time we helped Clemson, Judge Bell had been my mentor for years.

Judge Bell told Clemson that King & Spalding would perform its legal work for the school pro bono because he believed the documents of a public official needed to be accessible to people at a public institution. To express his appreciation for King & Spalding's work, Bill Atchley, the president of Clemson at the time, invited Judge Bell to attend the Clemson-Georgia Tech football game and a pregame reception with important political and businesspeople from around the state. Judge Bell accepted and asked if the invitation was open to the other lawyers who worked on the matter. President Atchley said it was, so Judge Bell invited all the members of our team to go to the game and reception.

Clemson is a couple of hours from Atlanta. Judge Bell said he'd drive Mrs. Bell, Betsy, and me to the game—a generous, characteristic offer from the judge. And if there was one thing I knew, it was that we wouldn't be riding in fancy foreign luxury. We'd make our way in a comfortable, if not unassuming, green

Buick sedan. It was his car of choice because he thought expensive foreign cars were a waste of money, and Judge Bell trusted Hix Green, who owned the Atlanta Buick dealership. Hix always dealt with him fairly, he said, and he wanted honest people like Hix to stay in business. Honesty—something Judge Bell valued most.

The reception at President Atchley's home was attended by a who's who of South Carolinians. Both of South Carolina's United States senators were there, as well as most of the congressional delegation and other state political leaders. Heads of South Carolina corporations were present. Famous athletes who'd graduated from Clemson attended.

Five South Carolina state troopers were posted near the door when we entered. Judge Bell saw the troopers gathered in the foyer, went to them, and introduced himself. I also walked over, said hello to the troopers, and then proceeded into the reception. An hour later, I glanced at the door and saw Judge Bell still talking with the troopers. As we left, I asked him what they'd talked about, curious about what caused him to spend so much time with the troopers rather than the other dignitaries at the event. He said they discussed the challenges to law enforcement in the country and the need for more funding to do their job well. They talked about their families. In Judge Bell's eyes, these were the people who had real stature. They were the ones who gave their lives to serve and protect. And this reminded me that Judge Bell valued others for who they were, not the positions they held.

We headed for the game, and as we neared the stadium, we were immersed—figuratively and literally—into Clemson's colorful football culture. Clemson's school color is a vibrant, maybe even a bit gaudy, shade of orange. When Judge Bell saw this orange tsunami moving toward the stadium, he said, "Clemson has done great things for the dye industry in South Carolina." Judge Bell had a knack for capturing the essence of things in pithy but dead-on quips unembellished by unnecessary rhetoric. He knew the value of reducing the complex to something simple, and he knew how to word the truth about it for maximum effect. It was one of the things lawyers, clients, and his friends loved and appreciated about him. Simple, unadorned truth—something he valued it in all things, especially in practicing law.

The Clemson Tigers throttled Georgia Tech that afternoon. I can't remember the score. What I remember is watching Judge Bell live out his everyday life values. These were the values for which he was known, and he embodied them in every situation. He believed he could advance the public good by donating his services to help a school provide a place for the public to access the papers of a United States senator. He believed in loyalty to those who earned his trust, and he proved that by buying cars from Hix Green. He lived by his belief that all people were important by spending a morning talking to law enforcement officials instead of movers and shakers. He cared about their work and their families. He offered insights that were unique and communicated them uniquely. He searched for the truth. He knew his values, and he aligned with them.

Aligned Lawyers Sometimes Buck Conventional Wisdom

Aligned lawyers create the capacity to be aligned, and how they live is an alignment model for the rest of us. Among the most aligned lawyers I know is Ralph Levy, a law partner who taught me a practical lesson in how to protect my objectivity.

Ralph's office was next to mine for a number of years when I was a mid-level associate. We worked on several cases that centered on hard financial disputes. He had a keen mind for numbers. He was the only lawyer in the firm capable of representing, and understanding, actuaries in complex actuarial disputes.

At the end of one day, I walked into his office to find him poring over a pile of financial documents. I asked what he was doing, and he said he was trying to decide if it made more sense to pay off his mortgage and invest less while he did, or to keep his mortgage-interest deduction and continue to invest at the same level he had for years. He admitted the analysis was harder than he'd first imagined, and he was going to ask his accountant for help.

A few weeks later I asked Ralph how he was doing on his mortgage pay-off analysis. After talking to his accountant, he said, he'd concluded that it ultimately made the most financial sense to continue to take a mortgage-interest deduction. But Ralph told me he ended up asking himself what reasons, other than financial ones, might support retiring his mortgage debt. One consideration swayed his opinion. He decided that by paying off his mortgage, he would remove a major need to generate income when he was in his sixties. By removing the need for income, he could better analyze whether he wanted, rather than needed, to stay at the firm in his later years. Ralph's decision demonstrated his alignment to his values. He valued the freedom to pivot to other work if the time came, and he acted accordingly by getting rid of his mortgage debt, even though the move didn't make traditional financial sense.

Ralph was the managing partner at King & Spalding and often spoke to various internal groups about the firm and the law practice. He once wrote:

> It was my custom to welcome new, equity partners re-
> garding the relationship between how they manage their
> personal affairs and the autonomy a lawyer needs to be
> able to exercise appropriate judgment. I entreated them
> to treat their colleagues fairly, to take care of the long-
> term interests of the law firm, and to enjoy a satisfying
> career. I "preached" this message because I believe the
> way one lives their personal life is directly tied to how
> they act professionally. That is, living life in a financially
> reasonable way allows a lawyer the freedom to provide

objective advice and judgment without the pressure to create income to fund a life too fully leveraged financially. The goal of my advice to younger lawyers was to encourage them to maintain their personal, financial and professional independence, because that is what is required for a lawyer to engage in the practice of law successfully and to service clients fully.[1]

I've thought a lot over the years about Ralph's decision to retire his mortgage. It was the way Ralph taught me about aligning my personal values with law practice, even in the face of strong external business pressures. It was one of the reasons I chose Ralph as one of my alignment models.

Following Ralph's lead, I chose to pay off our mortgage a number of years ago. At the same time, I decided to downsize to ensure future independence and autotomy. In those decisions, here's what I found: living without debt is liberating. Debt can be retired not just by creating more income but also by downsizing personal expenses until the debt is paid off, and, for young people, this includes student loan debt. It is a common approach used by aligned lawyers who value their autonomy and independence, lawyers who want the freedom to pivot to a practice that better aligns to their values if the time should come.

Aligned Lawyers Are Intentional about Staying Aligned

Let me tell you a little more about Frank Jones, whom I mentioned earlier. His accomplishments are legendry. Besides arguing cases before the United States Supreme Court, he served as president of the American College of Trial Lawyers (an

---

[1] R. Levy, "On Autonomy and Professionalism," in *A Life in the Law: Advice to Young Lawyers*, eds. W. Duffey Jr. and R. Schneider (ABA, 2009). Every young lawyer—no, *every* lawyer—should read this chapter written by Ralph.

invitation-only organization of the most successful lawyers in the country), and served as president of the Supreme Court Historical Society. (This is not an exhaustive list of his accomplishments, of course; such a list could fill this book.) How he lived is the best example of his values.

Frank lived in Atlanta during the last decades of his professional life, but returned to his hometown of Macon every weekend to teach Sunday School. Frank loved to teach, and not just on Sunday mornings. He often taught values from his office in Atlanta as he managed younger lawyers and served clients and colleagues. He was passionate about the law and how he could use it to serve others. And as long as I knew Frank, he aligned his practice with teaching and serving those around him.

Clients revered Frank because he was honest and had the courage to educate them on the law and tell them when they were wrong. He was candid with them when he told them they should consider a settlement, even when he knew that advice was painful for the client to hear. He'd also fight valiantly if he believed his clients were right. That is why a financial-services client retained Frank to handle its appeal of a dispositive motion on a usury case, and he invited me to help.

Frank labored through the appeal record and determined the bank had done nothing wrong. We were on a tight briefing schedule, and I worked long hours because the case was important. Frank was in his sixties at the time, and, as the younger lawyer on the case, I knew it was my duty to spend the lion's share of the hours on the file.

As we neared our filing deadline, I sat at my office desk in the hour just before the sun came up. I was putting final touches on our appeal brief. I had driven to work in the dark, proud of the long hours I'd put into the brief, thinking that Frank would appreciate my effort. The draft brief before me, I reached for my coffee. When I did, I noticed my telephone message light on. It was a call from Frank. He'd had a thought about one of our arguments and wanted me to consider it as I edited. The message was left at 5:00 that morning—an hour before I got in. It was consummate Frank: dedicated to serving his clients and committed to excellence in the work he performed—cores values to which he adhered.

Frank thought about his cases all the time, always looking for the right solution for the clients who entrusted their cases to him. As a result, he worked more hours than most of us because his clients deserved it, and he did it because excellence required it, not because he could bill more.

Months later, Frank called a few lawyers to his office to talk about a case. None of us were assigned to it, he just wanted some input on an issue. He told us that a lawyer in our firm was on a flight from New York to Atlanta and had found an envelope left on a seat by a lawyer who represented the opposing party in a case he knew Frank was handling. He delivered the envelope to Frank because the heading on a memo in the envelope showed it related to Frank's matter.

Thinking the memo might have been a communication from opposing counsel to his client, Frank said the lawyers working with him on the matter were debating if they could read it. Some claimed that zealous advocacy, a core ethics principle for lawyers, supported Frank reading the memo, particularly because it came into their possession legally and could be deemed "disclosed" by opposing counsel. Another lawyer on his team argued the memo might contain privileged and confidential communications, and that it was disclosed inadvertently when it was left on the plane. She argued the memo should not be read. Frank wanted input from us and asked for our opinion on the issue.

After listening patiently to what we each had to say, Frank said our comments confirmed his initial decision to return the envelope and the memorandum to the lawyer who left it on the plane. He gave two reasons for his decision. First, he thought the memorandum was, at best, inadvertently disclosed, and that there was authority which at least implied the contents could not be disclosed to his client or used in the case. His second reason, though, had more weight. He said it was his obligation to fight based on what he was entitled to know in a case. He said, "We win on the facts, not on information which we had no right to receive."

Frank called his client and told him he intended to return the envelop. After hearing Frank's counsel, the client agreed. In a note returning the envelope, Frank told opposing counsel that neither he nor anyone else at our firm had read the memo, but that the lawyer who left the memo on the plane should review it carefully to determine if there was anything in it that was required by the federal rules of discovery to be disclosed. He instructed the attorney to be more careful with his work product in the future.

For Frank, honesty, integrity, and fairness were central to his practice of law. Further, because he valued teaching younger generations, he invited us into the learning experience. Frank's values were more important than any strategic advantage he might have gained. His alignment with those values didn't allow him to claim an unearned and undeserved competitive advantage. Aligned lawyers allow their values to guide their practice. They are not motivated by status, influence, or money. They do not give in to win-at-all-cost tactics. They believe practicing law is a noble profession in which they have the honor to serve others. They align their behavior accordingly.

Look hard for your Judge Bell, Ralph Levy, and Frank Jones and allow them to serve as your living alignment examples. Watch them closely and you'll see how invigorating and fulfilling it can be to practice law when your values and those of our profession are your true north.

But before we look at how the nuts and bolts of a properly aligned practice, let's take a deeper look at the things that can disrupt and interfere with our alignment.

Chapter 5

Alignment Disrupters

"Should you find yourself in a chronically leaking boat, energy devoted to changing vessels is likely to be more productive than energy devoted to patching leaks."
—*Warren Buffett, investor*

"The world as we have created it is a process of our thinking. It cannot be changed without changing our thinking."
—*Albert Einstein, theoretical physicist*

I joined King & Spalding as a litigation associate in Atlanta in 1981. We had great clerical support at the firm, and I shared an assistant with another associate. We turned work around quickly, at least for that day and age. I sent what I drafted to opposing counsel and clients using the United States mail. The mail provided what we used to call a quiet period—the three days before the receiving party received what we sent.

One day an announcement was made about a company called Federal Express which offered overnight delivery. Lawyers were enthusiastic about the service, which allowed for time-sensitive materials to be delivered the next day when picked up the night before. Overnight delivery was expensive, of course, but the expectation was that it would be used only when something had to be received the following day. We didn't think the service would be used that often.

When we first started using FedEx, there were only a couple of FedEx envelopes in the lobby each evening, but it didn't take long before there were stacks of FedEx containers. Soon, there were more boxes than there were overnight envelopes. The number of overnight deliveries grew as UPS, DHL, and even the USPS entered the market. Packages were now picked up throughout the day. Over a noticeably short period of time, use of an overnight delivery service became the norm. That, of course, meant lawyers and judges received an ever-increasing volume of letters, pleadings, and boxes of document the day after they were sent. These expedited deliveries created a new urgency in litigation practice. The quiet period gone, the tyranny of the urgent set in. Lawyers, judges, and clients began to believe that if you received something the day after it was sent, you should respond to it the same or the following day. The pace of litigation quickened, and with it tension and stress.

New technology also developed that allowed attorneys to create and revise documents faster. First there were "word processors," which recorded documents on magnetic cards. Documents stored on "mag cards" could now be edited without retyping the entire document. Copies could be made by reprinting the document. These early mag-card machines were a benefit to lawyers but a burden to our staff. The machine could only display about twenty-eight red LED characters in a tiny horizontal window. Finding the place in a document where edits needed to be inputted was hard, and inputting edits was harder, because you could see only a small number of words in the LED window. My assistant didn't mind one or two edits to a document. More than a couple risked a revolt. We skirmished often.

Word processors gave way to computers. Gone were the LED windows. Now, both lawyers and assistants could type documents and view full pages of them on a computer screen. Editing was easy, and changes could be made promptly and efficiently. Documents could be, and were, edited up to the minute they went out the door. But the endless editing and reorganizing of documents created still more work and more stress.

As if overnight delivery weren't enough, delivery times were further reduced with the advent of the facsimile machine. Now you could send a letter or pleading electronically, and it would be in opposing counsel's hands within minutes. A response was possible the same day, so faxes soon replaced FedEx as the most routine means of transmission of documents drafted on a computer. The pace of practice got faster.

I felt the effect of all these changes and even took advantage of them. On a couple of occasions in acrimonious litigation I weaponized the fax to fight faster to keep opposing counsel off balance—to prohibit them from getting an advantage. That brought increased tensions with counsel on the other side of a case, and I wasn't alone. Tensions increased between all litigants as creating and sending materials became quicker and easier. And then came email.

Email cut out the middleman and connected lawyers directly to one another. It became the litigator's dread, allowing for near-instantaneous connection. Terse and sometimes regrettable communication was just a few keystrokes away, inviting impulsive, and too often thoughtless, careless, and regrettable responses. The angrier the initial communication, the more careless and callous the response. Communications became more vindictive and ugly as increased delivery speed reduced litigation to an ignoble night street brawl.

Aligned Lawyers Resist Outside Influences

These "technological advances" in word processing and communication create unhealthy practice environment that lead to stress, anxiety, and sometimes even depression. They account, in part, for the reason why many attorneys are less fulfilled, and in many cases, miserable, as practicing lawyers. The speed at which lawyers are required today to generate work and to communicate disrupts, and in many cases, prevents alignment.

Aligned lawyers use technology but do not let it rule their lives. They control their pace of practice. Admittedly, there are court deadlines, emergencies, and client demands, but the day-to-day rhythm of practice is up to the lawyer. They don't allow new technologies to induce them to litigate at an unreasonable pace that is unfair to an opposing lawyer, their client, or themselves. Aligned lawyers are courteous and respectful to opposing counsel, respect that they are juggling other cases and trying to serve all of their clients well, are committed to family and personal priorities, and engage in litigation as a truth-seeking, not a leverage-generating, process. They use advances in technology to benefit the litigation process, not to bludgeon or burden others, and their values govern the pace of their work.

If there's one thing I've learned about good litigators in my career, it's that they really want a more reasonable and thoughtful pace in litigation practice. They want things to move forward efficiently, but they also crave the capacity to think about what they are doing and why. I learned this lesson years ago from one of my partners.

I was the associate assigned to a case, and the partner handling it wanted a plan for discovery. I was to draft it. It was an important step in the case, so I worked long hours to get it done and gave it to the partner a couple of days later. I occasionally checked in, asking if he had any comments on the plan. One day, after asking yet again for his comments on the plan, he said that judgment often requires space to exercise it. He said he liked the plan but wanted some time to consider how the client might receive it. He also wanted to think through how it fit with our obligations to the opposing party in the case and whether it was the most cost-efficient way to go about the discovery process. He then said, "Slow down. I know you want to move the process forward, but we also want to make sure we are moving in the right direction when we start. This is not a race."

These words changed the way I practiced, and they changed the way I handled cases as a judge. While on the bench, I held phone calls with lawyers to discuss schedules. Sometimes we talked about discovery, sometimes motions, other times about preparing for trial. Lawyers expected me to impose a schedule on them, but that was not my practice, except in cases of unreasonable and disagreeable lawyers. Instead, we discussed the process for discovery or motion practice, and then I'd ask, "What would be a reasonable time for you to provide what we agreed on?" There was always a pause, followed by a review of calendars. They'd discuss obligations in other cases, trials they had scheduled, their vacations with their family. I'd then propose a date that accommodated these concerns but kept the case on track. They were often relieved by the accommodation, and I'd remind them that if something came up and they needed more time to complete the tasks, we'd find it, so long as I had enough advanced notice and a further extension was justified and reasonable.

A practicing litigator has the same power and authority. When discussing scheduling with opposing counsel, an aligned lawyer will ask, "What is a reasonable date to complete the task?" They don't demand a response by next Tuesday or try to dictate the pace of litigation in an attempt to gain an advantage. They don't bait opposing counsel into terse written exchanges or voicemail messages. Rather, they remove artificial expectations and reach consensus. They set the pace and tone for the process. When they do, it releases tension and an atmosphere of cooperation settles in without sacrificing progress or efficiency.

A Different Priority in Communication

It's tempting to use technology, often emails, to discuss the case with opposing counsel. Because we seek to avoid unpleasantries, real or perceived, it seems easier to write someone than to talk to them. But honest communication, and ultimately understanding, most often happen when people talk with each other, and the best way to do that is in a face-to-face meeting. Of course, we don't do that much these days, unless it is in an internet-aided virtual conversation. But the prominent reason we don't communicate in person, or on arranged virtual conferences, is because it is easier to shoot off an email or text and move on to something else. We offer all kinds of justifications. Internet-based communications are less expensive (though what we really mean is that it is more convenient and comfortable: you don't have to schedule a meeting time or drive to a meeting location). We find it difficult to discuss hard issues in person (which is to say we're conflict avoidant). But technology of any kind always interferes with our opportunity and ability to understand people, to understand their motivations and the nuances of their communications. It can be a barrier to our ability to connect on a meaningful level. Personal meetings remove these barriers and help us develop trust.

Years ago, I met with a lawyer to talk about his response to a motion. He wanted an extension of a deadline he had missed by several days, and I told him we needed first to get together and discuss how the case was progressing. I agreed to go to his firm, which seemed to surprise him. When I arrived, I was ushered into a conference room and he came in shortly after. We talked about the nuts and bolts of the case and what needed to be done. We eventually turned the conversation to the deadline he'd missed, and for which he now requested an extension. I asked if something had happened that caused him to miss the deadline. He explained that his son was struggling in school and that he and his wife were concerned. They had seen a medical professional for help and were trying to decide how to get him in a better learning environment. I could see he was distressed.

When he finished, I told him I had sons and understood his anguish. I told him not to worry about the missed deadline and asked when he could get the information to me. He offered a date, which I said was fine, but that he if he needed more time, he should let me know.

The discussion, understanding, and solution I proposed would never have happened in an email exchange. Good communicate involves words. Better communication involves openness, authenticity, understanding, and empathy. Those are possible when the people communicating are face-to-face in a room or, if necessary, on a screen. Lawyers need to embrace face-to-face meetings.

The Client as an Alignment Disrupter

You might consider an opposing lawyer to be unaligned, uncivil, and obstreperous. But a lawyer's unreasonableness and perceived incivility may be driven by their client.

A colleague once told me about a discussion he had with a client in a high-dollar commercial dispute. My colleague was a hard-nosed advocate. In his case, he'd completed a risk-cost analysis. He evaluated the legal claims in the case, the chance of the client winning at trial, and the expected cost of litigation. He told his client that he believed the client had, at most, a 50 percent chance of winning, and that the case was bound to be expensive. Considering these odds, he thought the client should consider settling.

The client was unmoved. "Hell, I've made a lot of business decisions with much worse odds," he said. "Let's press on," he continued, "and don't talk to me about settlement again." His opposing counsel at various stages of the case urged my colleague to consider a resolution before trial. But his client had been clear, we take no prisoners. Fight until we die was his instruction. My colleague was required to take positions that did not seem reasonable or necessary, even if none of them were ethically prohibited. My colleague's alignment urged him to resolve a case, but he knew his client ultimately would object to any settlement amount. Alignment—his values—cried out for a different course, but his client declined his aligned advice. Sometimes the duty of zealous representation of a client conflicts with the alignment of a lawyer.

A client's demand that a lawyer chart a path different from the one the lawyer recommends always has the potential to disrupt alignment. The aligned lawyer assumes an obligation greater than simply advising a client what they can and cannot do. The lawyer's responsibility is to advise their clients regarding what they *should* and *should not* do, based on a greater sense of justice, fairness, and an application of the law. But after that advice is given, a lawyer, within reason and the constraints of the law, should assert the claims, defenses, discovery demands, arguments, and strategies of his clients. And sometimes this is true even if the lawyer thinks the claim, discovery request, argument, or position is not in the client's best interest.

Aligned lawyers know that resisting a client's instincts may require tough conversations. It may even create tension in the attorney-client relationship. But candor and judgment are the hallmarks of good representation and aligned lawyers. Sometimes there is risk in delivering legal advice, including the risk of irritating a client. Client engagement, however, is key to seeking successful results, and aligned lawyers can confront a client because they have worked hard to develop trust with them. In a way, this illustrates how shared professional values, such as zealous representation, can butt up against the personal values of a lawyer, such as avoiding developing a reputation for unreasonable refusal to resolve a matter or structure a deal.

This conflict may suggest values that are at odds. But the shared values of the profession—the values we promise to adhere to when we become officers of the court—take precedence. A lawyer who wants to align to their personal values may have to

ALIGNMENT DISRUPTERS

give way to a client's desire to advocate a dispute that may not, for the lawyer, seem wise. A lawyer's duty, however, is to the client, even if it causes tension in a lawyer's alignment with his personal values.

My close friend Larry Thompson told me a story of a case he'd worked some years ago with Judge Bell. Their client was the subject of a government investigation, and Judge Bell and Larry were at the client's office to discuss the case and decide how to proceed. Judge Bell made his recommendations, and the client's in-house counsel countered with how the company wanted to respond to the government's inquiry. Judge Bell listened carefully to the response then told him he disagreed. He explained why he believed it was wrong and would alienate the government, was not proper, and would lead to adverse results. In-house counsel stood firm on how the company wanted to proceed. Judge Bell, believing the course of action inappropriate, gathered up his papers, put them in his briefcase, pushed his chair away from the table, stood, and said, "Come on, Larry, it's time for us to go." The client representatives were silent—maybe a little shocked. But the decision to leave emphasized Judge Bell's conviction in the recommendations he made, recommendations he believed were in the company's best interest.

Before Judge Bell could leave, the client persuaded him to stay, and the discussion of options changed. The executives and in-house counsel knew his values as a lawyer and his integrity as a person. They trusted Judge Bell and Larry, and if two of the finest lawyers were willing to walk out on a case, they knew they should reconsider their advice. Judge Bell's alignment and courage led the way, and at the end of the day, the client followed his advice and was better off for it.

Judge Bell knew his personal and professional values and always stated them openly. His values dictated how he lived and the advice he gave. He acted on what he believed and wouldn't bend to clients when they wanted to pursue questionable or

65

improper strategies. He did that all his life, and as a result, he developed deep bonds of trust with his clients and opposing lawyers. It is why he was appointed as a United States circuit judge, was asked by a president to serve as attorney general, and was asked by a different president to represent him in a congressional investigation. Judge Bell's reputation earned him significance beyond measure. It is the outcome achieved by those aligned.

So, what does a lawyer do if a client dismisses your advice, if they try to cajole you into pursuing a course of action that would pull you out of alignment? What if the client wants to embark upon a course you believe the client should not take because it's improper, unethical, or simply reckless? A lawyer must have the courage to stay aligned to their values and beliefs and to stick by their conclusions. In those moments, a lawyer might run the risk of losing a client or may have to incur expense to unwind the relationship. The willingness to run that risk requires integrity to engage a values-based, well-aligned practice.

A wise, older lawyer told me once over a beer in Summit, New Jersey, that the ultimate act of a lawyer's independence is when a lawyer fires a client. I withdrew from the representation of only two clients in twenty years of practice. Only after our relationship was terminated did I fully appreciate that my connection with those clients was not based on our trust of each other, and that issue had to be confronted and resolved. Alignment sometimes requires hard choices, including terminating a client relationship.

A Final Word on Ending Incivility

Lawyers don't need more seminars or books on civility. They need to cultivate it. Civility happens only when lawyers value it. Lawyers are the masters of how they relate to opposing counsel. The aligned lawyer commits to regulating their conduct, exercising restraint, and carefully and thoughtfully communicating. The receipt of an unpleasant or unfair email in the early evening doesn't require a testy or rude response an hour later. A proposal by an associate to serve opposing counsel with a motion a few days before opposing counsel goes on vacation so she has less time to respond should not be allowed by the partner supervising the case. Tit-for-tat litigating seldom accomplishes anything. Personal meetings and conversations over the phone are more likely to smooth rough edges in a relationship.

One final thought. Let's abandon the belief that the willingness to accommodate others is a character flaw. From time to time, it might be in our best interest to concede an issue in order to accommodate an adversary. In some cases, the concession may simplify the case. But there may be times when opposing counsel might request a scheduling change to attend a family function, schedule a vacation, or deal with a family emergency. Opposing counsel may need grace when one of his family members is struggling. These accommodations may not be required, and making one may give up some perceived advantage, but when appropriate, and when client interests are not compromised, granting extensions and reprieves builds civility in the practice. Accommodation more often shows confidence and strength than it does weakness.

In the end, all of us have to confront and avoid alignment disrupters. Disrupters such as technology, an obstinate opposing counsel, and client demands might challenge our alignment and impede our ability to serve clients successfully, and we must resist them. Why? Because serving clients well is what aligned lawyers do best. Let's consider how aligned lawyers cultivate client relationships.

Chapter 6

Serving Clients Successfully

"You can make more friends in two months by becoming interested in other people than you can in two
years by trying to get other people interested in you."
—Dale Carnegie, writer and lecturer

"If only you'd ask, I'd be happy to say
I wish you would do things more often my way."
—Felice Wagner, A Client's Poem

In October 2019, FTI Consulting, an independent business-ad-
visory firm, released a report entitled "General Counsel Report:
Corporate Legal Departments in 2020."[1] The report captured
survey data from chief legal officers about the future of the legal
profession and what corporate clients want from their lawyers. It
includes three noteworthy findings:

- 66 percent said lawyers need to know the client's business
  better
- 53 percent said law firms need to consider alternative billing
  arrangements
- 38 percent said lawyers need to focus more on the practical

---

[1] https://www.ftitechnology.com/resources/white-papers/the-
general-counsel-report-corporate-legal-departments-in-2020

These findings illustrate outside counsel's failure to fully understand the clients they serve and how that failure undermines a strong client relationship. Consider it this way: if 66 percent of the general counsel say lawyers need to know more about the client's business, that means that only 33 percent of the lawyers serving corporate clients know enough about the company they are serving. And that begs this question: How can you represent someone if you don't know who they are, where they've come from, and what they do? Further, how can a client trust a lawyer who doesn't have the time or interest to care about who they are?

Aligned lawyers care about and invest in getting to know their clients. They take time to understand the client's background. They seek to know the corporate history, its leadership, its culture, its product offerings, the markets it serves, its involvement in the community, and its management and workforce. If the attorney is serving an individual, he'll do his best to understand the client's work, career, family, values, outside interests, and hobbies. Aligned lawyers know that strong relationships best serve their clients. Understanding who they serve is critical to their representation, and relationship building is an important and interesting aspect of practicing law. Relationship building makes serving the client more personal and more rewarding. Ultimately, it results in a different approach to practice.

Aligned, relational lawyers advise differently, bill differently, and engage clients differently. Fundamental to this different practice approach is this understanding: we are given the privilege to serve, advise, and counsel others, a privilege that is intensely personal because it almost always has a personal impact on the people being served. Aligning to this truth informs the way we interact with, advise, and advocate for clients. But what does that look like?

Establishing Trust Relationships with Clients

It is a lawyer's duty to develop client trust. A person who finds themselves in a dispute or in need of legal services generally enters a system that is foreign, confusing, and uncomfortable. The same is true for businesses and their leadership. They likely don't know the demands of trial. They may not appreciate the effort involved in preparing for a discovery deposition or the anxiety experienced during it. They may not believe they've done anything wrong and may be incensed at the process of having to navigate a lawsuit. Because legal processes and principles are the lawyer's domain, a lawyer is able to explain, guide, and quiet the nerves of a client in the litigation process. That, however, is only possible if the client has deep trust in the person representing them.

Establishing trust with a client who is an individual is no different than developing any mutually respectful and trusting relationship. You need to know something about their life story, their work, family, aspirations, and hopes. This helps you understand how a legal issue affects them and gives you empathy for their predicament. It also helps you create a connection with the client, which forms trust. It's this trust and empathy that helps the lawyer dispel client angst and encourages cooperation.

Developing trust with a commercial, institutional, or government client is really no different than doing so with an individual client. While the case may be by, or on behalf of, an entity, it is the people at the organization who ask for legal help and who are involved in the legal process. In representing an entity, you may principally interact with the client's in-house counsel, if it has one, but behind the in-house attorney is a businessperson whose division has been affected by, or accused of, wrongdoing. If there is no in-house counsel, you interact with the people who run the company. Either way, there will be hushed break-room conversations in which employees or managers wonder if someone in the company made a mistake, and, if so, whether the mistake or misconduct will affect the entity's viability, cause the company's stock price to take a hit, or affect its employee 401(k) plan. Others may wonder if they will be drawn into the controversy, and when they are, they'll wonder why. Although a lawyer cannot—and likely does not need to—counsel everyone at an entity, he or she should try to develop trust with those directly involved in the dispute and maybe those at the organization who stand to suffer the greatest impact of the case, including its management.

But outside of understanding the client's background, how does a lawyer develop trust? This is a great and important question.

In most cases, earning a client's trust takes time and develops by a process. There is a logical set of steps. First, a lawyer should ensure the client understands the nature of their relationship with a lawyer and the legal protection afforded by the attorney-client privilege. An attorney should help the client understand how this privilege protects the confidentiality of their communications, which allows the parties to be candid and honest with each other. As the client becomes comfortable with this protection, even the worst facts can be openly shared with the lawyer. These honest and candid discussions allow the attorney to best serve the client.

Trust Relationships Lead to Results

Next is the development of trust. There are times, of course, when a lawyer must give difficult assessments and advice. There are times when the lawyer has to hear hard truths from the client. There may be arguments from time to time. But if there's a mutually trusting relationship, each will understand these confrontations are the product of each wanting to ensure all issues are considered so that sound decisions are reached.

I once represented a woman who became the subject of a criminal investigation. She was a widow, raising eight children and holding down a full-time job at a staffing company to support her family. One morning before dawn, federal agents showed up at her home to execute a search warrant. They believed her employer was enticing foreign students to come into the country illegally to staff businesses and thought she was involved. She was devastated by the accusation and told a family member about the visit. That family member asked if my firm would help her.

I took the case, and we met to discuss what happened. I asked about her family, how she was making ends meet for her children, the kind of work she did that provided her income, and her current job duties. I asked how she was holding up during the investigation. I then asked about the search and how the agents treated her during the execution of the warrant. She immediately became emotional, describing how terrifying the early-morning confrontation was for her and her children. Regaining her composure, I asked about her children and how they were handling what was happening to her. She went into detail about the great character and success of her kids, and their support of her resolve to confront the accusations. When the meeting was over, I went to our firm management, told them she had few resources and real exposure, and recommended that we represent her pro bono. The firm agreed.

Over the following weeks, she and I had several meetings discussing the facts, and I quizzed her at length about what she knew, testing her credibility. In our discussions we often talked about her family, the impact of the case on her children, and the toll the matter was taking on her. The government was aggressive, and the allegations serious. She was scared to death. After several weeks, we discussed whether she should submit to an interview with the Assistant United States Attorney handling the investigation, rather than appear before the grand jury. The Assistant United States Attorney (or AUSA, as they are more commonly called) investigating the case was tough but fair, and an explanation of her limited duties might persuade the government not to indict her. I told her she was a credible, trustworthy, and sympathetic witness and because of that I trusted her.

We talked about the AUSA's request to interview her in lieu of a grand jury appearance. She asked whether there were any risks, and I gave it to her straight. It wouldn't be easy. If she fumbled with her answers, she might appear to be hiding something. But I assured her she could do it, and told her I'd be present at the interview, even though I couldn't give any input. In the end, she said she trusted my assessment and agreed to meet with the AUSA handling the case.

The day of the interview, we sat in my office, and I again walked her through what to expect. She was understandably nervous and in despair, wondering what might happen to her and her children if she was indicted. But she never backed away from her account of her job and what she knew and did not know, maintaining, as she had done from the start, that she did not know whether her employer was engaged in illegal conduct. She was prepared to tell the government the truth, she said.

The interview lasted a few hours. She was authentic and certain about what she knew and didn't know. She was emotional at times, but her account of her work and duties never varied.

A few days after the interview she asked when we might know something about her status. Probably in a few days, I said. She then said that during our meetings, I said things to her she'd only let her father say. I'd been tough on her, she said, but she knew I had only her interest at heart. She said I was kind though I never relented in pressing her with questions to find out what she knew about her boss's actions. Because of the trust we developed, she never doubted that I believed her, and she never questioned my advice.

A couple of days later, I received an update from the investigating AUSA who told me the government was not going to pursue a case against her. As we ended our conversation, he asked me to wish her well.

Months later, a package arrived at my office. It was a beautiful wooden box. In it, my client included this note:

> I had my son make this for you. I thought you'd like it since you enjoy woodworking. I told [him] it had to have clean, classic lines, with wood that had depth, warmth & character like you. I think it will be a good place to put your treasures. Your goodness to me is my treasure.

The box sits on a bookcase in my office and has since I received it. In it is her note. It reminds me what happens when you build a relationship of trust with your client. It also reminds me of the warm sense of fulfilment that comes with serving a client well.

My client entrusted her life and her family to me, and I worked hard to earn her confidence. It is what makes our profession a solemn one, and it was this trust that enabled the effective, efficient, and successful conclusion of this matter. Trust is the watchword in successful client relationships. Aligned lawyers, those whose primary aim is to serve others, work hard to forge a binding trust relationship, because those bonds of trust are key to achieving right and just results.

Understand Personal Impact

Real litigation has real impact on people. Remember that always. It is not just a game of who wins or loses. Be aware of, and understand, the personal impact of a case. I learned this lesson in a very real way in a case where a company was in the midst of a civil-government investigation into its lending practices. I represented the company, and the impact on it was potentially significant. It put pressure on the company's financial reporting and stock value and on certain responsible individuals in the company.

The investigation uncovered problematic conduct by a particular manager. I was at the manager's interview by a lawyer from the office of the attorney general of Georgia. Represented at the interview by his own counsel, the witness admitted to some troubling conduct, and, as a result, a decision was reached to place him on paid administrative leave so the company could evaluate the nature and impact of what he'd done. The company asked me to have the employee's lawyer return the employee's business credit card, office-entrance key card, and the keys to his company car. I talked to the manager's lawyer and relayed the company's request.

The employee's lawyer called me at home that night. He said he wanted to be the one to tell me that his client had committed suicide. The items the company had requested were found on his kitchen table, accompanied by a note which simply said: "Please give these to Mr. Duffey."

That moment drove home a hard truth: what lawyers do is hard because it affects very real people and their lives. To represent anyone well, a lawyer must have empathy for those he represents.

The following day, I had a hard discussion with my client. We talked about how to respond to the human tragedy suffered by their employee and the impact of his death on his family. We discussed how to announce the death to company employees and the sequence of these communications. We talked about how to communicate about the event to the state lawyers investigating the case, and how to offer assistance to the manager's family. All these conversations were hard. My client listened to my advice because we'd developed a deep trust relationship. The client representatives understood there were both legal and human implications and that I understood those implications as an outside counselor. And together, we made our way through that tragic death and its legal ramifications.

Trust Once Gained Must Be Sustained

Trust initially earned must be fostered. While a client may trust you and your advice, trust should be cultivated during the entire course of a matter. This is achieved by telling your client what has been done and why, what additional work is planned, what advances have been made, and what problems have arisen. Litigation, including contingency cases, usually involves substantial cost, and it has an effect on the day-to-day life of a client. Trust is cultivated by providing a client with detailed bills showing what services were performed, by whom, and what is charged for them. Periodic reports on case developments deepen trust that you are engaging the litigation on behalf of your client and are willing to report on developments—good and bad. The latter are the hardest. You may have represented your client in a deposition of an employee who did not do well testifying. You may find a letter produced in discovery that damages the case. You may have an employee deliver to you a report she wrote that affects the issue of causation in a matter. Whatever it is, if it affects the case, the client needs to know about it. It is your client's case, not yours. Your job is to act objectively and communicate with your client candidly. So, even though giving periodic development reports can be a bother, it is better to meet your duty to keep a client informed than to have the client tell you later that he or she was surprised you had not told them something earlier. And while this may be stating the obvious, significant developments, good or bad, are best reported in person.

A few years ago, I represented a major real estate firm in a complicated matter. There was an important principle my client wanted preserved by filing suit, and the CEO was actively involved in managing the case. As we approached the time of trial, he told me I had not been "aggressive" enough and that I'd been too polite with opposing counsel and the "jerk" he represented. I told him we were in a good position, that we'd have our day in court, and that I couldn't bully the other side into surrendering. I told him we needed to let the process work because we had a good case.

A couple of days before the trial began, I got a call from a senior partner in our firm who told me he had just gotten off the phone with the CEO of my client. The CEO had asked if I had the will to win. My partner responded by telling him that while he might not agree with my style, he would like my results. My colleague then said, "Tell me I wasn't wrong."[2] I went over the case and our litigation strategy again with him in detail, and he commented that he thought we had laid the right foundation, probably enjoyed the judge's favor, and would likely win. Sure enough, we tried the case and won.

I ran into the client in an elevator lobby a few years after the case. I knew he had retired as CEO, and I congratulated him on a successful career and his impact on our city. He thanked me and said he'd been watching my career too. "I should have contacted you years ago," he said, "to tell you I regretted going over your head to a senior lawyer in your firm." He explained that the case I handled meant a lot to him and he didn't want to lose. He then said, "While I didn't want to lose, after the case was over, I realized that it was far more satisfying to win well and with dignity. You did that." He finished, saying that he was glad I didn't let his backdoor call to my partner affect my resolve to win. He

---

[2] There is a lesson here about being a good partner. The partner in our firm and I had a good relationship, and we had worked on some matters together. He was a transaction lawyer and the partner responsible for the firm's relationship with the client I represented. His very first instinct when he got the call was not to accept the client's evaluation but to defend the work, reserving the right later to talk to me about the case and upcoming trial. Trust among partners is as important as trust with clients.

later realized, he said, that everything I had done in the case was in the interest of his company.

He then told me that after the case was over, he met with the opposing party and had a long discussion about their business relationship and the trial outcome. Ultimately, they mended fences and did some business together. Then he made this comment: "For someone younger than me, you had the wisdom to take a longer view of the case. As old as I was then, I didn't think I could have a long view. What I should have known is that when your time is short, relationships should be preserved and not destroyed. The way you litigated for us helped me preserve a business relationship I was in the process of destroying."

As lawyers, we should always take note of wise insights, including those offered in elevator-lobby conversations. You don't need to take an overly aggressive approach to be an effective advocate, even if the client might want you to. Truth is, that's not how you ultimately build trust. You build trust by serving your client with the long view in mind, and it is the long view that earns a client's respect.

Relationships Are Cultivated with Care

The need to develop a strong trusting relationship with a client applies to lawyers at all levels, including young ones. Afterall, the nuts-and-bolts work gets done by those with lower hourly rates. But as a young attorney, building these kinds of strong personal relationships with an organization's key leaders is not always realistic. Young attorneys often do not have as much of an opportunity to interact with decision-makers at a company. But young lawyers have different relationship-building opportunities and should act on them.

If you're a young lawyer, look for those opportunities open to you to build strong client relationships. Take document searches, for example. The search for documents responsive to requests to produce is typically assigned to an associate, and often occurs in the client's office, or in the case of individuals, maybe in their home. A lawyer needs the help of his client counterpart to help identify where responsive documents are kept. The assignment is a unique opportunity to build client relationships and trust at lower levels of an organization. You do that by serving the client well. While you're visiting with the client during the review, explain the nature and importance of the case. Help the person you're working with understand relevant legal issues that might affect the production. Explain how improper or inadequate document production can significantly damage a case and influence a court's opinion about a client's credibility and trustworthiness. Let the client know the search is an important role in the litigation. Answer truthfully and candidly questions that come up. Ask them to explain the meaning and context of documents you find. The goal is to develop a collaborative team working on an important task—a key to building trust.

In a breach of contract case in which I was involved as an associate, my job was to collect documents that might be responsive to document requests. A young manager in the risk management department was my client liaison, and it was a job he did not want. He didn't know much about the case, and I knew the document search would go best if my liaison understood the litigation and if we developed the search strategy together. I set up a meeting in his office,[3] suggesting we review the case and the document requests together.

---

[3] How a lawyer views his or her role in litigation affects even the smallest decisions in a case. Lawyering is a profession of service to another for what a lawyer is reasonably, if not generously, compensated. The question then is what serves the client best? Is it better client service to schedule a meeting in the client's office, the lawyer's office, or to discuss the matter in a phone call? That may depend on the nature of the meeting, what needs to be discussed, whether documents will more effectively be reviewed face-to-face, the space required for the

Complaints are wordy, technical documents, and I decided to summarize in a chart the facts alleged and the claims asserted. But before I explained the chart, we talked for several minutes, sharing personal information. We found we were close in age and both trying to establish ourselves where we worked. We both had sons in Scouting, and that shared experience went a long way in forging a connection. It was a valuable initial conversation.

I turned to the claim and fact chart, which helped the client liaison understand the serious nature of the case and the claims against the company. He began to see his collection responsibility as one that was entrusted to, and not dumped on, him. We next discussed how the company retained documents and developed a strategy to search for responsive materials in the company's general files and databases and in the files of individual officers and employees. Our plan included a timeline for the search, a list of those whose files would be searched, and how we would minimize the impact of the search on their duties.

After our collaboration, the general counsel of the company said he appreciated the integration of his staff with ours, and he concluded that we had developed the least disruptive process to efficiently meet the client's obligation to produce documents. Over the years, my client contact on the search advanced in the company and became the go-to guy on legal issues and litigation management. I became his go-to lawyer, an unexpected development of our work together. If I had gone into the company ordering how the search was to be conducted, without taking the time to connect and explain, I would have created tension and distrust. That would have been unproductive, certainly wasn't necessary, and could have resulted in less work coming my way.

---

meeting if one is held, and where the client prefers to meet. Client service requires these kinds of thoughtful considerations.

Client Development:
Dinner, Drinks, or Aligned Connection

Building a client relationship requires diligence. Once established, it should mature and strengthen. To most lawyers, client development means drinks, maybe dinner or a concert. These are safe and easy options that don't fit well in our current culture, and haven't for a while. In fact, I think many lawyers and many clients believe dinner, drinks, and events are more of a burden than a benefit. It is not lost on a client that dinner at an expensive restaurant is paid by someone, maybe them. They also tally up the cost of being away from their family and friends. Aligned lawyers have, for some time now, developed client relationships differently.

Client development should be about getting to know your clients, and there are different, better ways to get to know them other than by wining and dining. The aligned lawyer's objective is to create connection, and there are times when a dinner may, for the right reasons, do that. For example, having dinner with a client from out of town, who is away from their home and family, is a gift of time to someone who might otherwise be alone.

What's more, I generally don't believe "entertainment," as normally practiced, is all that important in establishing goodwill with clients. That said, I admit that inviting a client to an exclusive or prestigious event may build a bond with some. After all, few people have access to tickets to the Masters or a private concert by Beyoncé, and inviting special clients to those kinds of exclusive events makes an impression. Still, I question the advantage of "big ticket" entertainment. In my experience, thoughtful invitations to events tailored to the interests of those invited are better. Aligned lawyers know that client relationships are best cultivated when event invitation is personal.

Consider this outside-of-the-box example. A local lawyer who had an excellent relationship with our firm had a keen interest in cars. Each year, the National Hot Rod Association holds the Southern Nationals drag races in Commerce, Georgia. I had been a fan of drag racing since the time I was a kid, when my dad took me to a drag race when we lived in California. There, I was introduced to Shirley Muldowney and Big Daddy Garlits, drag race icons; but that is a story for another day. The Southern Nationals is an elite race and a true cultural experience. That year, Shirley Muldowney was on the race schedule, so I invited the lawyer who loved cars and his sons to visit the Saturday session of the race with me and my son. We had a grand time and the boys loved the day.

This lawyer, to this day, is fond of telling his drag race story to his friends and colleagues. And often, as we've discussed other matters, that Saturday has come up. We forged a connection that day, and that established what became a long and rich professional and personal relationship.

The point is, when engaging in client development, aligned lawyers create innovative, unique, and personal experiences because they know and understand their clients. Clients appreciate the chance to know their lawyers on a deeper level, and aligned lawyers know the best way to show appreciation for legal work is to provide a client with an opportunity for respite from their daily toils and to discuss other important things in life, like children and their interest in community activities.

A trusting, collegial, and professional relationship between a lawyer and a client is central to the practice of our profession. Cultivate and guard these relationships. Make sure you're advising, treating, communicating, and relating to them in ways that align with your personal and professional values. But don't just stop with developing client relationships. Work hard to develop an aligned approach to the other relationships necessary to the practice of law. What are they? Let's take a look.

Chapter 7

Relating to Opposing Counsel Productively

"As a peacemaker the lawyer has a superior opportunity of being a great man."
—*Abraham Lincoln, American president and lawyer*

"The lawyer on the other side, or the judge, is not the enemy, but a fellow traveler on the journey toward discovering the correct legal answer."
—*Justice Clarence Thomas, associate justice, United States Supreme Court*

When I was on the bench, I told lawyers they should not terminate a deposition if a dispute arose but should call me. I said I'd make myself available to resolve their dispute, even if it meant I had to take a break in a court hearing. Over the years, lawyers took me up on my offer.

One day, in the middle of a hearing, my deputy courtroom clerk slipped me a note. Two lawyers in a deposition had a problem, and one of them refused to allow the deposition to proceed unless their dispute was resolved. I told the lawyers in the hearing I had to take a short break to address a problem in another case and went to my chambers to take the call. When the attorneys were on the line, I asked if the court reporter had an audio backup of the deposition. He did. I asked him to play the tape back, beginning about two minutes before the dispute arose. I wanted to hear how the dispute developed, and I wanted those at the deposition to hear what I heard. The tape was played. When we got to the point where the deposition was stopped, I told the court reporter he didn't have to play the tape further. And I let the silence settle in. What I and everyone else on the call heard was nothing short of shocking. Lawyers yelling at each other, foul language, character attacks, and a physical threat. I didn't have to say much. The tape said it all.

Before I could say a word, the attorneys apologized for their conduct and told me that if I gave them a few minutes, they could work out their differences. They muted their speaker, and a few moments later came back on the line to tell me that they'd resolved the issue. I never heard from them again on the matter.

I wondered then (and still wonder now) how lawyers could treat each other as they did in this case. I suspect some of it was the pressure of litigation. In some cases, lawyers mistreat opposing counsel and witnesses because they've learned that bullying a lawyer or an opposing witness might give them a strategic advantage by creating confusion about the testimony being given or by distracting the witness to interrupt their train of thought. Sometimes aggression is a calculated obstruction tactic. And in some cases, lawyers act out this way because they are just plain mean.

Whatever the reason for incivility toward a colleague, it is wrong. Aligned lawyers don't obstruct the orderly process of litigation, and they don't justify uncivil conduct. Aligned lawyers realize that each instance of incivility represents a block that builds their reputation. They know reputations carry a lot of weight with other lawyers and judges. Poor ones erode trust and good ones earn credibility and respect. Aligned lawyers work hard to establish reputations of civility, honesty, and integrity because this enables success.

But how do aligned lawyers build a respected reputation when the stakes of a case are high and a proceeding acrimonious?

The goal of any attorney should be to learn the facts of a lawsuit and then participate in the process of seeking a fair result. Sure, every attorney wants to win, but they know that exercising professionalism and integrity in seeking justice is more important than their win-loss record. Aligned attorneys view wins and losses differently. A win in a weak case may be to accept a fair, albeit small, recovery to help a client cover some expenses to pursue a claim. Aligned lawyers prioritize treating others with fairness and dignity and don't excuse their bad behavior on the pressure of practice or the unreasonable demands of their clients. They know that belligerence and disruption of the truth-seeking process is not zealous representation of a client, is inconsistent with the shared values of the profession and is not necessary to achieve a winning result.

Professionals Align to their Values

In 2004, hundreds of cases were consolidated before me for processing in a multidistrict litigation proceeding. Each plaintiff in these consolidated cases claimed a defect in a hip-implant device caused them injury. The allegations were serious, and the damages alleged were high. It was the kind of high-pressure and high-verdict case in which a lawyer can sometimes lose sight of civility. That didn't happen in this piece of litigation. The lawyers representing the parties were accomplished and set the gold standard for advocacy and professionalism. They cooperated without compromising their duty of zealous representation.

How? Here are some examples.

In discovery, the defendants requested the medical history for each plaintiff. This is the kind of discovery request that often results in a donnybrook, with the plaintiffs claiming their medical privacy is threatened by the very company that injured them, and the defendant claiming the plaintiff seeking significant damages disclaims the privacy of their medical records and conditions. It is the sort of request that encourages legal brinksmanship and often requires a court to intervene.

Not in this case.

The plaintiff lawyers believed their clients were seriously injured and understood their obligation to provide significant medical information. They knew that the information requested was reasonable and believed it would help prove the injuries each patient suffered. So, they concluded, the defendant was entitled to do the same analysis they had.

The defendant's lawyers knew they needed information about the plaintiffs' injuries to adequately defend their client, but they also knew the information they wanted and needed did not require overreaching discovery. The lawyers for the parties discussed the medical information needed and how to produce it. They agreed on the scope and form of the production, and then asked me to formalize the agreement they'd reached by entering an order. I did.

There were occasional disputes about discovery, but these too were resolved in a reasonable way. Each time a dispute arose, counsel for the parties conferred and, at my request, summarized their position on each dispute in a letter. I used these summaries to prepare for a telephone conference to resolve their differences. If I couldn't, I told the parties they were allowed to file motions and briefs to explain the issues I needed to consider so I could enter an order they could appeal. The dispute letters they submitted gave me clear, concise, and cogent descriptions of their positions, and in every instance, I found each had a reasoned position in their disagreement. They simply needed my help to decide what was fair. They did not posture or embellish the truth. They simply wanted an objective, outside voice to resolve their differences. When I told them my decision, the dispute was over and the case proceeded uninterrupted. Discovery motions were never filed. The time and money saved was significant.

At some point the parties began to talk about settling the cases. Each had their reasons to resolve the litigation, and each had facts that made settlement challenging. In exploring a resolution, they were open with each other about what they required for their clients to conclude the case. They shared information candidly, trusting the information disclosed would not be misused if negotiations failed. Throughout the case, these lawyers built their reputations for cooperation and transparency, and because they trusted each other, their settlement discussion resulted in a global settlement of a case seemingly impossible to resolve.

I also witnessed the lawyers battle in the courtroom when one of the cases was tried before a settlement was reached. Even when things got tense, the lawyers were respectful and polite to each other. They never compromised their duty to their clients. Their civility before the jury and before me enhanced their trial presentations and was applauded by the jury. It proved what I knew: Aligned lawyers know that being rude and contentious does not win cases, the facts do. Aligned lawyers know their reputations are important and often result in successful litigation results.

You're the Master of Your Reputation

I've practiced law for a long time. I've worked with lawyers, against lawyers, in consultation with lawyers, and as an advisor to lawyers. I've managed lawyers and presided over them in cases they litigated in my court. I've watched them in environments where the stakes were high and the stress overwhelming. I've spent time with them socially. Here is what I've learned as a lawyer and a judge.

Reputations are everything in law practice. They can facilitate or impede a case, impact the cost of it, determine practice and litigation success. They influence whether a lawyer is, or is not, hired by a client. They impact whether a lawyer is accepted into a partnership. They can determine if a lawyer is asked (or told) to leave a firm.

As lawyers, our reputations are built over time and are based on what others think of us, particularly the lawyers we litigate against and the judges we litigate before. Our reputations are built by what we write, our conduct in court, the way we treat other lawyers, and how we act in public.[1] The best reputations are built by lawyers who are well-aligned.

If you extend dignity to others, believe that your word is your bond, practice candor as a virtue, and act civilly as you seek fair results, you will align how you act with these values. When you're up against an uncivil, disagreeable opposing lawyer or a difficult judge, you'll continue to abide by these principles. In doing so, you'll earn a reputation for stand-up character and as a go-to lawyer for your clients. What's more, you'll earn a good reputation with other attorneys, especially those who also are well-aligned.

This leads to another observation. Opposing counsel can have a particularly significant impact on a lawyer's reputation. In fact, opposing counsel may be the most powerful reputation influencers. Having the opportunity to see how you act and treat people under stressful circumstances—whether you act honestly or only self-servingly, whether you accommodate or obstruct the truth-seeking process—opposing lawyers are in a unique position to offer their opinion of you because they've seen and experienced your character under pressure. Throughout the course of

---

[1] Subtle conduct can tell you a lot about a person. Does a person with a title introduce themselves by title or their name? In an elevator lobby, when the elevator opens, does someone push ahead of others or wait until others are on before entering. At the grocery store, does someone park in the fire lane to be close to the entry, or in a space in the parking lot further from the entrance? How a person acts tells you a lot about what they value—in these cases how they view their importance in relation to others.

your career, occasions might arise for opposing counsel to share their opinions of you in ways that might disrupt opportunities. How? Here's an example.

Each time I was considered for a federal appointment, I had to complete a lengthy questionnaire that had a section in which I had to identify cases I handled and the opposing counsel against whom I litigated. I knew that during the vetting process, the people I had identified would be interviewed and that they, in turn, would be asked for the names of others who knew me. That second layer of opposing counsel would then be interviewed. These multiple interview layers provided a fair account of my reputation.

I know the process well because over the years I have been interviewed about lawyers that were opposing counsel in my cases. I gave honest opinions about them, most often giving strong endorsements of the candidates and their reputations. In one case, though, I did not. Apparently, others had the same reputational reservations because the candidate wasn't appointed.

Once established, a lawyer's reputation, whether good or bad, sticks. It becomes the lens through which others view you, your competence, your character, and your trustworthiness. Your reputation will affect your practice, the results you achieve, and your ability to attract clients. It will affect your relationship with other lawyers, especially cocounsel and opposing counsel. Ultimately, it may affect whether you advance in your career and are fulfilled, or whether you find yourself fed up with your work.

What is irrefutable is that your reputation is primarily within your control because it is your conduct, your communications, and your relationships with others that influence what others think of you. Aligned lawyers know litigation success is affected by their reputations and is measurably determined by how they treat opposing counsel, juries, and the judge.

Avoiding Regret

Reputation-building is work that requires constant vigilance. When thinking about building a reputation, I'm reminded of an old saying that a close colleague, and former army ranger, learned while serving in the infantry. The adage, cleaned up a bit from the army version, is, "I can climb a hundred mountains and you won't call me a mountain climber, but let me screw up just once and I'll be forever known as a screw up." The moral of this saying? One lapse in character a reputation can make. Whether you suffer a lapse will depend on how well you are aligned.

Lapses in character can happen in the matter of a moment. In the heat of an argument, the desire to win a case, the hope of avoiding a bad ruling, or the need to feed an ego, we can make bad judgments and harm our reputations. Worse yet, in these kinds of character lapses, your client's or your firm's reputation also can be damaged. In fact, jurors have told me that while they find combative and rude lawyers in TV dramas entertaining, they are offended by similar tactics in a real court proceeding, including those in which they served in my courtroom. They've indicated that attorneys who respectfully and forcefully point out when an opposing lawyer is wrong help jurors understand the case and its evidence, but the attorney who disrespects opposing counsel or a witness erodes trust. That can be perilous to your client, your case, and your credibility with the court.

David Trachtenberg is a fine lawyer. For years he practiced at a premier law firm in New York. I was in private practice in Atlanta, and David and I represented opposing clients in a difficult piece of litigation. David and I had had day-to-day responsibility for managing the case for our respective clients. We litigated hard, maybe at times too hard, and often resisted whatever the other did. We sent communications late in the afternoon to disrupt each other's lives. We made normal discovery requests difficult and could be unnecessarily contentious. It was litigation hell, and I may have added most of the fuel for the fire. I made myself miserable as I tried to seek the smallest of advantages. I knew I wasn't litigating consistent with my personal and professional values—treat everyone with dignity, don't take advantage of others, play hard but fair. I was co-opted by the enormity of the case and the money at risk and had convinced myself that my obsession with winning justified the hard time I gave my opposing counsel, David.

David and I eventually helped resolve the case and, a few years later, left our respective firms. I went into public sector work, and David struck out on his own to start a small, respected, boutique litigation practice in New York. He's successful by every measure, and we've kept in touch. A few years ago, we reminisced about our historic piece of high-stakes litigation. He asked a pointed question during one of our conversations: "What exactly did we accomplish by the way we litigated?" I said I could only speak for myself, but I knew I had made our lives and litigation harder and unpleasant, and looking back, it had no impact on the outcome of the case. I told him I was sorry for the acrimony. We both regretted our contentiousness and agreed that it was a version of our earlier selves.

I wish David and I had cooperated more. If we had, we might have become better friends during the case instead of years after it was over. A little more candor and appreciation for the pressures we both faced would have built trust and understanding of the expectations our firms had of our performance. It would have encouraged more patience with each other without affecting our duty and desire to represent our clients well. What's more, it might have enhanced our reputations, something we each wanted. And for what it's worth, we both left our respective firms because we wanted to practice in environments that were more aligned with our values, values I had shelved as we fought with each other.

Reputation Repair and the Value of Humility

There will always be times when we don't treat people as we should. Unchecked and uncorrected intemperate behavior can cast us as short-tempered, uncivil, and maybe even arrogant and rude. But when your conduct goes outside the bounds of civility, admitting it and apologizing can prevent permanent reputation damage. In fact, it may even establish your reputation as one who exercises humility, who has the courage to admit your shortcomings—something often missing in our profession.

In a piece I wrote on civility a few years ago, I described two times when I needed to address my intemperance. In the first, I thought a lawyer tried to manipulate the discovery rules. In the second, defense counsel got angry about the position I was taking in a case when I was the United States Attorney, and he claimed I was grandstanding.[2] In both incidents I had misgivings about things I said. On both occasions I called the lawyers and apologized. One of those lawyers tells others how unexpected and appreciated was a call from the United States Attorney to mend a fence.

The best lawyers, especially aligned ones, understand that zealous representation of a client does not require engaging in reputation-marring conduct. They know that zealous advocacy, tempered with reasonableness and civility, is the bedrock of professionalism and is at the heart of a good reputation. They accommodate reasonable requests for changes to schedules for discovery. They work to forge cordial relationships with those against whom they litigate. They are candid about their views of the strengths and weaknesses in the respective positions of the parties, and they do so without exaggerating or being pompous. They don't participate in testy email exchanges or make grandstanding arguments during telephone conversations. They don't

---

[2] *A Life in the Law: Advice for Young Lawyers*, chapter 11, eds. W. Duffey Jr. and R. Schneider (ABA, 2009).

threaten to haul opposing counsel to the court to bully them into a concession on some minor, often feigned, dispute. They find ways to resolve differences and avoid unnecessary expense and court intervention.

How do you build this kind of reputation? By thinking about what others may say about you when they talk with other lawyers or what they may offer when they are called when you are being considered for an important appointment.

Your reputation is your legacy. Aligned lawyers build reputations that make them, their children, and their grandchildren proud. Their reputations extend beyond opposing counsel. Aligned lawyers command the respect of their staffs, associates, and fellow partners. Let's talk about them next.

Chapter 8

Aligned Colleagues

"The challenge of leadership is to be strong, but not rude; be kind, but not weak; be bold, but not a bully; be thoughtful, but not lazy; be humble, but not timid; be proud, but not arrogant; have humor, but without folly."

—*Jim Rohn, businessman, author, and motivational speaker*

"One of our values is that you should be looking out for each other. Everyone should try to make the lives of everyone else who works here a little bit simpler."

—Stewart *Butterfield, founder of the team-messaging application Slack*

After a few years on the bench, I got a call from the chief judge of our circuit. There was a delicate matter in another district, and all the judges had recused because of a conflict. A judge from another district had to handle the case, and the chief judge asked if I'd preside. I agreed.

I asked one of my very bright law clerks to work with me on the matter, and he was excited about the chance to work on a high-profile case. It was unique and contained challenging issues, and the press followed it closely. He worked hard on the case and did a sterling job supporting me on some unusual and particularly sensitive legal issues.

When the trial date approached, we talked about when we would leave Atlanta to get ready for the trial in Alabama. He said that he had been thinking a lot about the trip out of town. He and his wife, who had just given birth to their second child, were concerned about whether she could handle things at home while he was gone for a couple of weeks. He had concluded that he couldn't leave her alone with a newborn and regretted telling me he couldn't go. He had made an aligned decision, and I applauded him for it. Right?

Wrong.

I didn't take his decision well.

This clerk was the only one familiar with the case. He had wanted to work on it, even though it would take more work than our other matters. He had not told me that he'd be unavailable to travel if his wife delivered before trial. And so, my emotions oscillated between disappointment and being downright miffed. But knowing how hard he'd worked and how important his family was to him, I exercised restraint and took some time to think it through.

When I mulled over what to do, I remembered my second assignment in the air force. Two prosecutors were assigned to my office who were responsible for prosecuting felony cases in the southeast United States and Panama. Each of us had cases that required travel outside of our home base in Alabama. Betsy was pregnant with our first child and scheduled to give birth near the time that I was scheduled to try a rape case in Mississippi. As the trial date drew closer, and Betsy's delivery appeared imminent, I asked my boss if we could assign someone else to try the matter. He was scheduled to try a murder case, so he couldn't handle it for me, and we then discovered there weren't any prosecutors from another circuit who could fill in. He suggested that I ask the military judge and defense counsel if they'd agree to reschedule the trial for a few days after Betsy gave birth. They agreed. The judge told me to call him after Betsy delivered, and we'd then set the new trial date with defense counsel. That's what I did. After I called, the judge set the trial for the Monday after Betsy got home from the hospital. I was grateful to be home when Charles was born, though I regretted leaving Betsy with a newborn while I spent two weeks in trial in Mississippi.

Family and the families of those with whom I work are key values to me. Although it would be hard for me to transition the Alabama case to a new clerk, I remembered how I felt having to leave town just after my first son was born. I knew I needed to accommodate a request by the young lawyer if I was to align my behavior with my values. What's more, the accommodation allowed the clerk to align his behavior to his own values. In the end, I figured it would be a valuable accommodation for both of us.

I contacted my other law clerk, whom I had just hired. I told him I needed his help on a case that would be tried out of town. The trial would be challenging, and it would require his immediate attention to get up to speed on the matter as soon as he arrived in Atlanta. I apologized for tasking him with this new case just as he was starting, but I shared how his co-clerk needed to support his wife and children. He didn't see it as a burden at all. He said he understood the need for his co-clerk to stay home with his wife and new baby. He also made it clear he was excited for the chance to dig into trial work sooner than he thought he would in his new job. Working on trials was, after all, the reason he left private practice to clerk. Spending a couple of weeks in Alabama was, to him, an adventure, and he was enthusiastic about the opportunity. During the trial, he worked harder than he needed because he wanted to prove he was up to the challenge and because he wanted to provide excellent support.

More than a decade has passed since then, and I've stayed in touch with both of these attorneys. I've been actively involved in providing career input as they've navigated the profession and when both considered work outside of law practice. They've become close friends and often together call me to wish me well on my birthday. I'd like to think that is because instead of losing my cool years ago, the three of us made a collective, collegial decision to align to our values.

Aligned Lawyers Are Colleagues, Not Just Coworkers

Where and how you practice is important for lawyers. Both young lawyers and seasoned ones should find a place where they can align their values with their practices. This question will look different depending on career stage.

It takes time to discover what alignment looks like. Because of this, young lawyers don't necessarily know how to identify others who have similar personal and professional values. Young lawyers also don't have the experience or credibility to be choosy about where they will begin their practices. For them, it is naïve to insist on working only at a place they perceive is hyper-aligned with their priorities. A beginning lawyer's priority is to find employment that will expose him to good training in a good work environment, and where she can see how lawyers who have practiced longer approach their work. Working with other lawyers permits a lawyer to experience how aligned and unaligned lawyers engage the profession.

I found that in my early years of practice. As a young lawyer in the air force, I learned to spot aligned lawyers early, even if I wouldn't have exactly put it that way then. I worked with JAG officers who were dedicated to the mission of the air force and who wanted to give sound advice, both legally and practically. These military lawyers never griped about their military pay, and they found their work worthwhile.

I also met lawyers on active duty who counted the days before they could leave the service for private practice or griped because they felt they were undercompensated. They were not interested in developing young lawyers, and they looked for ways to move every given assignment off of their desks and onto someone else's. They tolerated their workplaces because they were biding time before they could leave for more lucrative jobs or could retire and collect retirement pay.

By watching these attorneys, I got my first glimpse at what aligned practices look like. I did my best to work with aligned lawyers because they put the time in to train me. They knew the long-term success of the JAG Corps relied on passing down the values of our legal work and the military mission. They also knew that if they aligned their conduct with their values in their present job, they'd have a better chance of aligning in their next assignment. They knew they'd be the most successful, most qualified candidates for private practice.

I loved my time as an air force officer, but because I wanted to litigate rather than manage a legal office. I decided to explore private practice. I took a few days of leave, and Betsy and I went to Atlanta so I could interview for associate positions at law firms.

My first interview was at a firm that had about sixty lawyers. It had an active litigation practice and a good list of clients. I was scheduled for personal interviews with several associates and partners. My first interview of the day was with a mid-level associate. He greeted me in the firm's reception area and invited me to his office. When we entered it, he reached behind to close the door. He asked me about our trip to Atlanta and a little about my experience in law school. We had a few minutes of small talk about my work. Then the interview took an abrupt turn. He paused, looked me in the eye, and said, "Don't come here." He said he'd reviewed my résumé, knew I had served in the JAG Corps, and tried lots of cases. He said I would get lots of offers, and then said, "Don't waste your time here."

Did I hear that right? He went on.

"I've worked here for a few years. I didn't mind the long hours or the quality of the work I had to do. The partners always said it would improve and that I'd be given more stand-up work soon. In my last annual review, I was the highest rated lawyer in my class. But no one ever gave me any real feedback about how I was doing."

I couldn't believe what I was hearing and couldn't fathom working in such a place.

He continued, "Yesterday we got an email that said the firm is merging with another firm, that the impact on us was not known, that not all of the associates will be invited to stay. The driving force behind the merger, I've been told by a partner, is the opportunity to make more money by expanding the cases we can attract, but I had to get that from a confidant. The firm has not even scheduled a meeting to tell us what's going on. This is not a way to treat us and I'm out of here."

Then and there, I probably should have terminated the interview at the firm, but I thought that would be impolite and that I ought to get a fuller picture, so I decided I'd finish my interview day. The concluding interview was with a senior partner. I hoped he might give me a better explanation of the merger, but before I could ask any questions, he said, "A lot of the young lawyers who interview here have been fed with a silver spoon. What's your background?" I was stunned by the question and the suggestion in it, but I gathered myself and answered. The questioned required a full response.

My great-grandparents were immigrants from Russia, Sweden, and Ireland, I told him. Neither of my parents could afford to go to college, so my dad enlisted in the navy in 1941, right after Pearl Harbor, and was given a battlefield commission during the Korean War. He retired after thirty-one years and then worked as an administrator in rural medical facilities. My mom started work at the retail counter in a department store, was promoted to work at the soda fountain, and then became a clerical worker at the Campbell Soup Company. Later she worked at the naval shipyard. My parents put all three of their children through college and grad school.

The partner didn't seem to care much about my background, assuming he even had heard it, and instead, asked, "Why do you think you'll fit here?" I knew I wouldn't, but I made some broad comments about my work ethic and my desire to do challenging work. I had concluded this firm was not a good fit. My values were unaligned with theirs, save one young lawyer who looked like he was on his way out. For what it's worth, not a single partner told me about the merger.

The next day's interview—at a different firm—was vastly different. When I arrived, I was met in the reception area by an associate assigned to take me to and from each of my interviews. I was given a list of interview times, the names of those I'd be speaking with, and the lawyers who would take me to lunch. The interviews were interesting, and we talked more about our experiences and backgrounds than about law-related matters. I met with two former JAG officers who told me the firm valued active-duty legal experience and found it translated well to private practice. One young associate told me he had attended depositions and recently was given the responsibility for drafting a deposition outline for a partner. The partner had given him a lot of feedback on the outline, and the discussion was a good learning experience. "It helped me understand the structure and process," he said. By the end of the day, I was having discussions with lawyers who were not on my schedule. These impromptu "in the hall" interviews showed the sincerity of the people I met and their interest in the firm's hiring process.

When the day ended, I went back to our hotel. When I returned, Betsy commented, "You look different today. It looks to me like you really enjoyed your time at this firm." I had. The lawyers I spoke with loved their work and loved their firm. It seemed to me more a collection of friends practicing together. They were engaged in the community and they talked a lot about things they had done with their children. They were interested in my time in the air force and my family. I aligned with their values and their view of the profession. It felt like a good fit, supporting my belief that whether you align with others often is accompanied by a gut feeling that a fit exists. I accepted an offer to be a litigation associate, and that's how I found my way to King & Spalding, ultimately spending twenty-two years practicing there. It was the place that prepared me for the public service appointments I was offered years later.

King & Spalding's culture was defined by the relationship between lawyers in the firm. In the years I was there, I shared personal and professional values with colleagues as well as members of our litigation staff. I didn't align with everyone, and it is unrealistic to believe that I would, but with those I worked with most, I shared their professional values and many of their personal ones. And they were people I trusted.

Looking back, I can define the characteristics of the firm and see why my values and theirs aligned.

Hard work and sacrifice were important. The matters the firm was asked to handle were often some of the most difficult in the country. Some of the cases we dealt with had the potential to affect a company's viability, and others affected the lives of people in profound ways. Others were precedent setting. The matters at the firm demanded a lawyer's complete and undivided attention because the firm's success was tied to the excellence of its legal work. As a result, the work ethic was strong.

Candor was important, whether with clients, opposing lawyers, each other, or the firm's employees. People may not have always liked certain business or management decisions, but they understood why they were made. Associates always knew whether or not they were doing well—they knew where they stood. A partner of mine told me about an associate who came to him one day to say his peers had plenty of work, but he did not. He said it was unfair that others were assigned cases while he was not often approached to work on new matters. My partner told the associate, "You should ask yourself why partners ask others to work on their cases but don't ask you. When you do that, try to define what other associates are doing that you are not. Maybe that will answer your question about why you are not asked to do more work." This partner taught this young lawyer to first evaluate his own performance and to later ask others for their thoughts on how they were doing.

Personal integrity was important. Lawyers were taken at their word. If they said they would do something, they were expected to deliver, and they were trusted that they would.

Judgment was important. Lawyers at the firm knew they could command significant billable rates because of their judgment, not just their technical skills. Good judgment was crucial. On one case, I was on a team responsible for investigating corporate misconduct to advise the client what, if any, discipline to mete out against officers and employees who had engaged in wrongful conduct. The partner charged with delivering our recommendations assigned two of us to present arguments for and against punishment. I was responsible for making the best case for significant sanctions. My partner was to make the best case for leniency—to present for each person what mitigated against an adverse action against them. We made our presentations to the entire team, and each member weighed in with their opinions. Together, we sorted out the best path and made the best judgment on what discipline to recommend.

Respect was important. It was important to extend it to courts, to colleagues, other lawyers, and people in all stations of life. It was common for lawyers to greet other lawyers and staff when walking through the halls. It was common to see a lawyer talking with our cleaning crew and security employees in the evenings, sometimes helping them with legal problems. Respect was modeled by lawyers in the firm. When I first started as a young associate, William King Meadows and Jimmy Sibley—

two of the firm's most respected partners (Mr. Meadows and Mr. Sibley to me)—came to my office and invited me to go to lunch with them the next week. Mr. Meadows was in his nineties and Mr. Sibley in his eighties. They came to work most every day. The following week, they picked me up at my office on Wednesday, and Mr. Sibley drove us to a seafood restaurant in East Point, Georgia. Mr. Meadows and Mr. Sibley were fond of the Wednesday oyster special. East Point was a struggling small city back then, but this seafood joint was legendary. Mr. Meadows and Mr. Sibley were treated with affection by the wait staff and owners, most of whom were minorities who knew these two men who had patronized their restaurant for years. And while we were there, neither Mr. Meadows nor Mr. Sibley acted as if he were important. In fact, you would have never known that Mr. Meadows was a King & Spalding founder and that Mr. Sibley owned more beneficial shares of Coca-Cola stock than any person in America. Respect was a core value for both men, and they showed dignity to the restaurant staff. In return, the staff showed their respect, borne from the way they treated others.

Honesty was important in all matters, including billing, pleadings, and briefs. We also were expected to be honest in how we communicated with each other and in our opinions about the firm and how it treated others.

Mentoring and training young lawyers were important. Some lawyers were better at it than others, but everyone found a way to contribute to the development of younger attorneys, which included helping good mentors find the opportunity and capacity to mentor.

Humor was important. It may have been the glue that kept us together. It was abundant. Each month we held a meeting of equity partners to discuss new business, financial matters, practice developments, special projects, and general matters of interest. I don't recall much about the meeting content, but I remember well laughing often during them. We didn't take ourselves so seriously all the time, and good humor and charity characterized our relationships.

Generosity was important. Year after year I was encouraged by the amount of money we collectively and individually gave to others. I always was humbled by the number of lawyers in the firm—partners and associates—who invested hours in providing leadership and service to nonprofits. It was part of the firm's DNA.

It was easy to align my values with my work at my former firm, because my personal and professional values aligned with the values of my King & Spalding colleagues. And though there were still hard issues to overcome as a firm and disagreements from time to time with partners, our mutual alignment helped us to deal with and resolve them. Our aligned values made the practice of our profession fulfilling.

How Do You Know If You Fit?

The values and conduct of an organization are often referred to as its culture. The legal department of a company, the legal staff of a government agency or legislative staff, the legal staff of a nonprofit, and a legal-services organization all have their own culture.

Political philosophy, religious beliefs, ethnicity, and socioeconomic status are not values, although they may indicate them. For example, a Muslim can have shared values with a Christian such as generosity, honesty, and charity, and these shared personal values, coupled with their shared professional ones, may be the foundation for a successfully aligned practice. The key challenge is to discover and evaluate the values held by others. It's usually harder when dealing with larger groups, such as law firms, legal departments, or agencies. Hard, however, does not mean impossible. It just requires a little extra work.

When you're trying to determine the values and culture of a place where you're considering working, talk with people who know the firm or practice and its reputation, the relationships between lawyers and staff, and how lawyers balance work with personal interests and obligations. Talk also with those involved in the hiring process. They'll want to share information with you. And talk privately with lawyers recently hired to find out if what they were told when hired compared with what they experienced when their work began.

I was responsible for hiring people to work in the United State Attorney's office in Atlanta. Of course, we looked for hardworking, honest, decisive, respectful attorneys. But there were other characteristics that were important to our office culture, but were less obvious. We tried cases, and in the process, worked collaboratively with motivated law enforcement agents to gather the evidence we needed. We only made honest presentations to the public. We did our best to practice humility, emotional steadiness, and a willingness to be evaluated based on merit and results. We were hard charging, but we also were collegial and helped each other with our cases. These values comprised our culture, and we looked for people who would fit into it.

I had a hiring committee screen the applications we received, and they flagged the four or five candidates they thought best qualified. I set up interviews with the candidates recommended. My interviews were unconventional. I knew their academic credentials and experience because I'd studied their résumés. I was more interested in understanding their background, what influenced their character and values, and how passionate they were about public service. The questions were always open-ended because I wanted them to talk. It was the best way to size up an applicant.

I usually settled on one or two people I'd consider hiring, and I often called their past employers. The purpose of these calls was to determine their fit—how well they'd get along with others, their work ethic, their judgment, why they were seeking a public service job, their demeanor under pressure, and, most important, did they really understand litigation. Were they intuitive litigators, and if so, were they self-starters? By the time I extended an offer, I thought I knew the candidate well enough to know if they'd fit in our office and align with our culture. And because of the work I put into it, more often than not, I was right.

The Billable-Hour Barrier to Collaboration and Connection

If lawyers practicing together are going to be aligned one to another, there must be mutual connection. In contemporary law firms, though, there is a single, powerful impediment to connection—the billing process.

Billing is what generates private-practice horsepower. It drives firm and individual-partner prosperity. And so often, success at a practice group is measured by profits because billing influences everything, including a firm's culture and the quality of lawyer relationships. How do I know? Because I've practiced law in contexts where the billable hour was not king.

When I was the United States Attorney, I served as the chair of the Organized Crime Drug Enforcement Task Force for the Southeastern United States. We identified the largest, most active transnational drug-trafficking organizations and tried to disrupt their operations. A group of prosecutors in my office worked exclusively on these task force cases, and there were prosecutors in other US Attorney's offices who focused on task force work. The attorneys assigned to these cases talked with each other all the time, which was essential to understanding the range and scope of drug-cartel operations.

One week I had visits from two task force lawyers from different United States Attorney offices to discuss a variety of strategic decisions and staffing issues. I noted they were both leading prosecutions of different organizations and asked them why one was devoting so much time to the other's investigation. One of the lawyers explained that his colleague needed an objective opinion on her approach to her case, and also needed help researching a few issues. He'd agreed to offer his time because the work was important and he wanted to help. There was no billable-hour barrier to their cooperation.

It is difficult to sacrifice your time this way when billable hours define productivity and profitability. It can be hard in private practice for a lawyer to help on a case he's not assigned to. And if the lawyer doesn't know if that time will be billed, he'll rarely jump on a case because performance isn't measured by the importance of the work. In a billable-hour world, performance is often tied to production. Billable hours too often silo lawyers within their own cases. I wonder how many good insights are lost because there are billable-hour barriers to collaboration.

So, if collaboration, for example, is an important value for you, look to work somewhere collaboration is encouraged. Collaboration might be harder to find at firms that bill by time increments. Some contingency-fee plaintiff firms are better at it, but even these firms rely on the litigation of multiple cases to generate profits, and plaintiff's firms know they have to hedge bets by juggling multiple cases since their income is based on successful resolutions. Siloing helps keep people focused, so they say, and it discourages helping on other's cases.

Firms, I think, are beginning to realize this barrier to collaboration and collegiality is not impossible to address. To do so, however, may require disrupting traditional billing systems. Consider this: a partner in a billable-hour firm has a sticky legal issue in a lawsuit associated with an industry with which he is unfamiliar. Say, for example, the case involves the electro-magnetic cutting process. He was a psychology major in college, but a young associate down the hall who graduated from Georgia Tech is familiar with the EMC process and thinks she could add expertise on the case, if she is allowed by her supervising partner to work on it. He knows the time required to help would take away from her other case responsibilities and negatively affect her billable hours. Understanding this, he proposes a solution: he will ask the partner on the case on which she is working if he will allow her to consult and allow her to bill for her time on his case and thus get credit for it in her aggregate billable hours. The partner for whom she works agrees because it benefits a colleague's case and because the Tech grad will be a better lawyer if allowed to work on matters that use her technical background.

Here two partners and a young lawyer value collaboration, value hard work, value excellence in their work product, and value good service to clients. As a result, they came up with a solution to put their values into practice, and suddenly work was more interesting, efficient, and fulfilling. That is the by-product of alignment. It is a golden thread in the tapestry of a fulfilled career.

It is important to work where your values fit with those with whom you practice. You must take these same values with you into the courtroom. But before you do, lawyers need to know something about the stress and strain that courts experience.

Chapter 9

Understanding Court
Stress and Strain

"Something happens to a man when he puts on a judicial robe, and I think it ought to. The change is very great and requires psychological change within a man to get into an attitude of deciding other people's controversies, instead of waging them. It really calls for quite a changed attitude. Some never make it—and I am not sure I have."

—*Robert H. Jackson, Supreme Court justice and chief prosecutor at the Nuremberg trials*[1]

"According to the U.S. Marshals Service, there were 4,449 threats and inappropriate communications against federal judges, prosecutors and court officials in 2019. In 2015, that number was 926. Over that same period, the number of threats investigated rose from 305 to 373, peaking at 531 in 2018."[2]

I was sitting in my chambers when my assistant told me two government officials were on their way to visit me. An attorney

---

[1] *The Justices of the United States Supreme Court 1789–1969*, 4 vols., eds. Leon Friedman and Fred L. Israel (1969): 2563.

[2] https://abcnews.go.com/US/threats-judges-increasing-experts-misogyny-problem/story?id=72061296

from the United States Attorney's office and the Deputy United States Marshal in charge of judicial security wanted to talk. The call was out of the ordinary, and I suspected it could only mean one thing: they needed to talk about a threat connected to one of my cases.

The Deputy Marshal arrived first. An Assistant United States Attorney who often appeared before me arrived a few minutes later. The AUSA began the conversation, reminding me that I had presided over trials involving two groups of defendants charged with running cells for a transnational drug-trafficking organization. Though the head of the organization was an American citizen, he'd fled to Mexico to run his drug operation but had recently been captured by Mexican authorities. News outlets reporting on the capture characterized him as a ruthless cartel leader who had a large distribution system and that his organization had been connected with tens of murders.

The cartel leader and his father-in-law were indicted in my district, and the Justice Department sought to have him extradited to stand trial in the United States. The Mexican government was not receptive to extraditing drug lords to countries where the death penalty might be imposed, because the death penalty is against Mexican public policy. Before agreeing to extradite any serious criminal to the United States, the Mexican government required assurance that the death penalty would not be imposed. In this case, the United States government had agreed, and the cartel leader and his codefendant were being flown to Atlanta to be prosecuted. I would preside over their cases.

After giving me this background, the AUSA left the meeting and the Deputy Marshal said she wanted to discuss security issues with me. Because of the high-profile nature of the case and the cartel leader's background and reputation for violence, extreme precautions were being taken in transporting the defendants from Mexico, and for their appearances in our courthouse. She described the security precautions that were being put into place. Because of the cartel cells' past activities in Atlanta, she noted the possibility that other members of the enterprise might be in, or travel to, Atlanta. Her office was actively looking into whether there was any identified danger to me or my family. She reviewed precautions we should take, and she promised to keep me posted on any security developments or threats.

The case progressed without incident, a credit to the Marshals Service and the security provided. Still, it was a stressful season, one that colored every aspect of my life for a number of months. The stress was a distraction at times and was always in the back of my mind. There's no doubt it made me more anxious, even if I didn't let on.

The Court's Different Environment

Federal judges perform their duties in an environment vastly different from the one lawyers and state court judges experience. Few people, including lawyers, fully appreciate the demands of the job. That's understandable. A federal judge interacts with counsel and the community mainly in the courtroom, and through the orders the judge issues. Lawyers may occasionally see a judge at a legal conference or a social event, but even in these informal settings there are restrictions on what a judge may discuss, especially pending cases. Judges are required not to make statements that could forecast their positions on issues that might come before them. Judges also don't share the very real threats hanging over their heads. To do so itself could affect the threat protections in place.

The relationship between a lawyer and the court also is formal and constrained because of the authority a judge has over counsel, clients, and their cases. A lawyer can't appear before a court without the court's authorization. Counsel must comply with the rules that federal or state authorities put into place to govern court procedures. They also must comply with rules of conduct that apply to the relationship between the court and counsel. There are rules that prohibit a lawyer from discussing a case with the judge presiding over it without the presence of opposing counsel. Some courts prohibit sending letters to the court, requiring instead that all communications be filed on the docket of a case so that it is available to be reviewed by opposing counsel and the public. The relationship is very structured to protect the integrity of the judicial process.

These controls are in place because of the role the judge plays in the system. The court's role in a case is as a neutral, restricting communication with parties and their lawyer to only when necessary. This prohibits one party from gaining an advantage over another and promotes the public's trust in the objectivity and fairness of judicial officers and proceedings.

This protection of neutrality and public trust begins in federal and most state courts with the assignment of cases to new judges. This random case-assignment system protects against parties trying to get a case assigned to a judge who a lawyer believes might favor their client or their position in a case, otherwise known as "judge shopping." It also illustrates how little control a judge has over his or her workload and the type of cases assigned. In fact, some understanding of case-assignment volume and mix shows how the judge's environment is so different compared to the environment in which lawyers operate. Whereas lawyers can pick and choose their cases, judges cannot. Judges have to take the cases assigned to them by the court clerk's office.

Neutral and Numbers

An aligned lawyer should understand what a judge experiences when he or she first assumes the bench, because this underscores the stress and strain of the job from the beginning. I'll use my experience as an example.

When federal district judges assume their judicial duties, they are assigned a "docket" of civil cases. In my district, the clerk's office uses the court's electronic docketing system to randomly identify civil cases from the docket of each judge to be assigned to their new colleague. At the end of this assignment system, the goal is for each active judge, including a new one, to have the same number of civil matters.[3] To accomplish this, each judge serving on the court is given a list of randomly selected cases proposed to be transferred to the new judge's docket. Each judge is allowed to keep one or more of the cases on this list for any number of reasons. Judges might keep cases because they've invested a lot of time in the case, the case is of particular interest to the judge, the judge has made rulings in the case and wants to manage the case consistent with their rulings, or because the case is on the verge of settling. Sometimes a judge will hold back easy cases in hopes that a case they want to be transferred will appear on a later list.

For each judge who holds back cases, the clerk's office produces a second list of cases to be reassigned. This list contains new cases equal to the number of cases that the judge holds back. The judge can withhold cases from this second list. If he or she does, the clerk of court creates a third list of cases. If cases on the third-round list are held back, a fourth list is created. This fourth list is final, and the cases which were not held back are assigned to the new member of the court.[4] This four-list transfer process

---

[3] Adjustments are made for those judges who have reduced caseloads because they have retired but continue with the court in what is called "senior status." They can elect to have cases from their docket reassigned to a new judge, but the number reassigned is reduced to account for their lesser caseloads.

[4] Because I assumed the bench after serving as the United States Attorney for my district, it was decided I would not be assigned criminal cases for six months to allow me separation from the office that would represent the government before me in criminal cases. To

did not exist when I joined the court in 2004. In those days, the number of lists that could be reviewed was not limited, and a judge could withhold cases for, theoretically, unlimited rounds, although at some point judges knew they needed to stop withholding cases from being transferred. The number of cases transferred to a new judge is significant. I was sworn in as a judge on July 1, 2004. On that day, I was assigned a docket of 286 civil cases. When I walked in that first day, I literally saw my 286 civil-case docket because 286 case files were stacked on the heating and air conditioning registers on the perimeter of my chambers office. The number of files was daunting.

The system for assigning newly filed cases also is random. Generally, as cases are filed, they are assigned to judges in the order in which the judges appear on a list. Judges do not have any control over the number or kind of cases assigned to them. Cases generally are assigned on the day they are filed. The immediate assignment of cases has a particular impact in districts in which all of the judges authorized to be appointed have not been confirmed by the Senate and sworn in. This happens often in the federal judiciary these days either because a president does not name a nominee to an open seat or the Senate does not process a person nominated to serve as a district judge. In fact, the Northern District of Georgia experienced a shortage of judges

---

compensate, some extra civil cases were assigned to me. I don't know now how many "extra" civil cases I received, and it didn't really matter. I accepted the assigned cases and got to work. The district currently does not assign any criminal cases to new judges. The criminal docket for new judges builds as they receive assignments in the regular assignment system for new criminal matters. This significantly delays when a new judge first has the opportunity to preside over a criminal trial, even for new judges with significant experience presiding over trials and appeals of criminal cases. The number of civil cases assigned to a judge greatly exceeds the number of assigned criminal cases.

in our district while I served. Our court was authorized eleven active judges, but for a number of years we were not at our full authorization. For several years we were short four of the eleven judges authorized.

When there is a shortage, the work impact is obvious. For example, during the period we were short four judges, the approximately one thousand cases that would have been assigned to them were assigned to the seven active judges and to senior judges who accepted new case assignments. The case burden, including the administrative duties we assumed as a result of the shortage, was at times severe. The demand for hearings and the issuance of orders were oppressive.

If a lawyer appreciates the work involved in being a judge, it might help the attorney to realize that just because he or she believes their case is the most important in the stack, it may not be. Patience may be required, something the judge will deeply appreciate.

Understanding the Stress of the Bench

Added to the sheer volume of cases is the difficulty of the issues presented. The mix of hard and less-challenging issues surprised me. I assumed that most of the issues in the cases assigned to me would be relatively straightforward and there would be a presumptively correct result. I expected 70 percent of my cases to fall into this category. The others I expected to be "gray area" cases. These would have more nuanced issues with less obvious outcomes but also have more intellectually challenging and interesting questions to decide. I estimated that 30 percent of the cases assigned would be in the gray area and thus the number of these hard cases would be manageable. I was wrong.

It didn't take long for me to discover that having to weigh issues from the perspective of all litigants was very different from advocating from the perspective of the party you represent. I found few cases were clear-cut, and that it was often hard to arrive at a just and fair result. Results weren't always intuitive. Sometimes the case law was not well developed, a unique question of law was presented, the facts of a case made it difficult to apply controlling authority, or the party had suffered damage, an injury, or requested a form of relief that made it hard to discern a fair and reasonable result consistent with the law.

There were times, though, when the cases were difficult because lawyers made them so. Sometimes they embellished, distorted or confused facts, misinterpreted or misrepresented legal authorities, or used rhetoric to disguise their reasoning. These kinds of strategies were put into place by two types of lawyers. There were those who did so unintentionally because of inexperience, poor legal training, hurried submissions, or incompetence. There were others who obfuscated to frustrate opposing counsel and sometimes to mislead the court. This second category of lawyers often engaged in calculating conduct to seek their preferred result at all costs.

The calculated conduct of these lawyers was motivated by variety of factors: a distorted view of the profession as one of gamesmanship; a driving ideological belief in a targeted result; the desire to generate a fee or justify a retainer; or, in rare cases, complete disregard for the integrity of the legal process. Whatever the reason for the conduct, I had to deal with these attorneys and take the time—often extended—to hold lawyers accountable for manipulating the judicial process. This diverted attention from other cases and created an additional layer of complication and stress. In other words, sometimes a case that appeared straightforward was not that at all.

As I worked my way through the cases assigned to me when I was sworn in, I discovered there were clues about how the lawyers intended to advocate, the quality of their written work, their cooperation or contentiousness, their reasonableness, and the credibility of the relief sought. I identified cases needing immediate attention—some had been pending a long time, others had important motions pending, still others had jurisdictional issues that needed to be addressed. Some cases could be resolved quickly, and I attended to them to unclutter my docket so I could focus on the more complicated ones. Removing delay-causing barriers became important to me, so each day I reviewed every new docket entry in my cases to identify problems. I used this information to decide on the management methods to efficiently process each case assigned.

I reviewed all newly filed cases to prioritize them. A complaint or a motion often helped me understand the seriousness of the claims presented. The preliminary report and discovery plan helped me understand how lawyers viewed the claims and defenses in the case, the legal issues in the matter, the complexity of the facts, and how much effort they intended to put into the case. I reviewed every motion filed to evaluate whether there was a reasonable ground for it. For example, I reviewed every motion to dismiss and the responses to them, which gave me the clearest view of the claims, their strength, and the competence and reasonableness of the litigating lawyers. This "early detection" management tool was invaluable. When I identified an issue that would delay or detour a case, I often set a telephone conference to resolve it. In this barrier-avoiding process, aligned lawyers cooperate with the court because it benefits the process and can directly and indirectly benefit them and their clients.[5]

---

[5] Cases filed by unrepresented, or pro se, litigants also complicate a docket. Some statistics for 2016 illustrate the burden. In 2016, a total of 5,687 civil cases were filed in my district. Of that, 2,200, or 39 percent, were filed by unrepresented litigants. A large portion of these were actions filed by prisoners challenging their convictions. That is an important right that defendants have in the criminal justice system, but they take time. What burdens a docket more are the increasing number of civil actions brought by other pro se litigants. In 2016, there were 929 cases filed by non-prisoner pro se parties. There are a variety of motivations for filing these cases. Some are filed to

Managing a civil docket is difficult and complex. But the criminal cases handled by a court are equally difficult and demand the first fruits of the judge's time for exceptionally good reasons. Because a person's liberty is often, if not always, at stake, and constitutional requirements must be met, judges give criminal cases priority. I've had to delay the hearings and processing of civil cases because a criminal case had to be tried. Civil lawyers didn't always appreciate the delay, even if it was unavoidable and necessary. Sometimes those civil attorneys shared with the court that they found the delay a serious disruption, adding to the stress of the job. The competing needs—those of a speedy trial for the criminal and those of a demanding civil docket—can, and do, frustrate the judge.

This kind of judicial frustration came up in my conversation with a state-court colleague over lunch one day. She recently finished a long products liability trial and was talking about what it was like to return to her other cases. She said, "When the trial was over, I returned to my office to see how far I got behind during the trial. I had six hundred cases on my docket, and I am trying to find how to get caught up." She had one law clerk, who was leaving, so the judge needed time to hire and train a new clerk to help her manage the cases on her docket. It takes time to manage six hundred cases along with the hiring process. Her anguish was apparent, and I felt for her because I've been there.

---

delay an adverse result. Sometimes it is because one or more lawyers approached to take the case declined to do so because they did not think the case had merit or sufficient verdict potential. In other cases, it is a way to retaliate against the person against whom the action is filed. Typically, the person filing the pro se action has little understanding of the legal claims they assert, and they do not identify any authority for the claims alleged. If they cite a statute, they often have not read it to determine if it applies. I know this to be true because litigants have admitted this to me at hearings I held in their cases.

Aligned Lawyers Extend
Understanding to the Court

The challenges that faced me and every other judge were similar. We had lots of cases, many were factually and legally hard, some meritless, some lawyers were difficult and had to be kept on a tight rein, and the list goes on. The time and resources available to judges to address all of the cases assigned to them are limited. On occasion, as I shared at the outset, the job is, by its nature, dangerous. Understanding the challenges judges face and the demands on their time and attention is important to aligned lawyers. Lawyers who are aligned recognize the environment in which the court works, the pressure judges are under, and are patient and exercise restraint when dealing with the court. They do not try to manipulate or unduly influence the court. They advance the most credible arguments in good faith and give judges the space they need to do their jobs. They abide by rulings, believing the court has done its best to achieve fair, just, and equitable results.

Understanding the stresses of the court should influence the way lawyers relate to judges and lead them to patient and thoughtful accommodation. But what does that look like in everyday practice? That's the next topic.

Chapter 10

Judicial Scrutiny of Lawyers

"A good reputation once broken may possibly be repaired, but the world will always keep their eye on the spot where the crack was."

—*Joseph Hall, English bishop, writer*

While serving as a federal judge for the Northern District of Georgia, I heard a motion brought by a company against a union member. The member (the defendant in the case) had made derogatory statements about the company to other union members, claiming the company mistreated union-member employees. The company wanted to enjoin the member from making any further statements. To complicate the matter, the defendant did not have a lawyer, while the company was represented by good and experienced labor counsel.

The defendant sat at his table and listened as the company lawyer made his concise and straightforward presentation. The attorney didn't use inflammatory words, but calmly and plainly stated the behavior the company sought to enjoin. The lawyer explained that the defendant was a good union member and a solid, hard-working employee. The company wanted to maintain a good relationship with him and wanted to let him have the chance to explain why he'd been speaking out against the company. With that, he finished his argument and took his seat.

I asked the union member to explain the statements he'd been making. Thanking the company attorney and me for allowing him to speak, he explained he was upset because he believed the company wrongfully favored certain union members over others, in violation of members' rights. The defendant acknowledged that the company had the right to take the action they had, namely, to enjoin his conduct, but he still thought it was unfair to do so. He explained why he thought he had a right to say what he did. Finished, he let out a sigh and said he appreciated the chance to explain his side of the story.

The company lawyer listened, then stated that the company would drop the lawsuit if the member agreed to stop making derogatory statements. The defendant said that as a result of the hearing, he better understood why his statements were wrong to make, and he agreed to the company's proposal. In those few minutes, the matter was resolved, all because a seasoned, respected civil litigator had used the court as a forum to seek a fair resolution instead of targeting a "winner take all" outcome.

If only all attorneys treated the court this way. The sad truth? They don't. A few years later, I presided over an insurance case in which the plaintiff filed an action for damages resulting from the insurance company's failure to pay a claim for fire damages to her home. There were some skirmishes during discovery, and the parties engaged in some fairly normal motion practice. Ultimately, the case was scheduled for trial.

I held the pretrial conference about a week before the trial date. The insurer did not dispute that the loss was covered under the insurance contract. The dispute, it said, was over the scope and cost of repairs required to fix the damage. The insurance company had calculated the costs of the repairs and the repairs had been completed and paid for, but plaintiff claimed she was entitled to damages far exceeding the repair costs paid by the insurer.

At the pretrial conference, counsel for the insurance company told me the plaintiff intended to present a previously undisclosed expert at trial to testify about a significant amount of additional damages plaintiff was claiming under the policy. The insurer argued that the late disclosure violated the rules of procedure, and the expert should not be allowed to testify.

The plaintiff's attorney's position was simple and self-serving: she now had an expert, the expert could produce a written report if he had to, and the homeowner wanted to start the trial as scheduled because the new expert was no big deal. It was clear to me that without an expert, the homeowner likely could not prove her case, and this might lead to an inequitable result. The homeowner was not a woman of means, and it wasn't her fault the expert wasn't disclosed by her attorney. I asked the insurance company's lawyer what he needed to prepare his case if I allowed the expert to testify. He stated he'd not object to the expert filing his report and testifying if the trial was postponed. He wanted time to depose the expert and counter-designate his own if necessary.

The request was reasonable, so I set a deadline for the homeowner to file her expert's report, set a date for the expert's deposition, and set the process for the insurer to counter-designate an expert if it wanted. I told the lawyers I was postponing the trial until the expert discovery was completed. The resolution seemed reasonable enough. Right?

Apparently not.

To say the homeowner's lawyer was livid would be an understatement. She failed to appreciate my decision not to strike her expert, thus preserving the opportunity for the plaintiff to present her damages case at trial. The lawyer dramatically gathered up her papers, threw them in her briefcase, and mumbled something about how unfair it was to delay the trial. She turned and abruptly left. This conduct was only a glimpse of what was to come.

At the second pretrial conference, counsel for the homeowner moved to exclude the testimony of one of the insurer's witnesses. The attorney for the insurer opposed the motion for various reasons, including the fact that counsel for the home-owner, during a visit to the witness's office, had surreptitiously copied pages from a manual in one of the offices. What's more, the attorney had photographs of certificates hanging on the hall-way interior to the waiting room. Plaintiff's lawyer tried to use excerpts from the manual and the photographs at the witness's deposition. Unaware of how she could have obtained these materials from his office, counsel for the insurer demanded an explanation. The witness accused her of trespassing on his property to get the exhibits. The homeowner's counsel responded, "I caution you on defaming me, because if you defame me, I can promise you it will not be good." She refused to state how she obtained the manual or the pictures.

Counsel for the insurer brought the issue to my attention. The way I saw it, how the homeowner's attorney obtained the materials affected whether they'd be admissible at trial, so I ordered her to file an affidavit stating how she'd come into possession of the photographs and pages of the manual. She failed to meet the deadline to file the affidavit, and after granting two filing extensions, she still failed to file it, so I sanctioned her for failing to comply with a court order.

The attorney appealed the sanctions and had the audacity to claim that I had violated her procedural rights by failing to give her notice of why I was considering sanctions. The court of appeals affirmed my decision, noting counsel had also misled the appellate court in her appeal, stating: "[Plaintiff's lawyer's] statement that 'the District court failed to notify [her] of a) the conduct that is subject to sanction; or b) the legal basis for said sanctions' is false."

To say this reinforced my already acrimonious relationship with the attorney is an understatement. Not only had she failed to operate with integrity and civility in my court, but she'd also attempted to mislead the court of appeals about my conduct in the lower court proceeding. Certainly, any trust that remained between the two of us was gone. The worst news, though, was that her client suffered the consequences. The attorney had shifted the focus of her case from the claims asserted to the conduct of the lawyer litigating them.

In another case, I held a hearing to confirm the appraisal of a piece of a land. At the hearing, each party offered the testimony of their own appraiser, both of whom offered a different property valuation. A partner and associate from a national law firm represented the defendant. The defendant's appraiser testified about his appraisal report. The lead defense attorney asked him about information in his report that he used to reach his conclusions. The other side objected that the information about which the appraiser was about to testify was given to him only that morning, and he hadn't had a chance to review it. He said the newly produced information and any opinion based on it should be excluded.

This late-delivered information had been in defendant's counsel's possession days before the hearing, and I asked why it wasn't delivered to the plaintiff until that morning. The partner representing the defendant beat around the bush, claiming the new information was not really important and did not prejudice the plaintiff. I asked again why it hadn't been delivered earlier. The lead lawyer finally admitted he didn't know he had the information prior to the hearing. He added: I hate to "throw Mr. Smith [his associate, whose name I've changed] under the bus, but he didn't make me aware of the information." The associate looked down at his pad, as if to scribble a note. Instead of owning the failure, the partner had deflected responsibility onto his employee.

That one move made a lasting impression. An attorney who would willingly and deliberately denigrate an associate, particularly in a case for which he was the lead counsel, was capable of disparaging anyone in order to shield him against criticism of his own conduct. His behavior put me on notice to be skeptical of his conduct in the future.

Months later, this same partner attended a luncheon I attended with my law clerks. He stood near me before the event and leaned in when I introduced my clerks to the out-of-town lawyer I knew well, who was giving a speech at the luncheon. When we returned to our office, my clerk told me that the attorney had come up to her later at the luncheon and asked her out. She declined the invitation, but she wanted me to know the conversation had occurred. She characterized the date request as inappropriate. That it was, and I added it to my inventory of the partner's questionable values. And though it would not keep me from exercising impartial judgment on future cases in which he might be involved, it caused me to view him with caution.

The relationship between counsel and the court is unique. The judge develops an impression of the attorneys from limited interactions, most often in official communications, case filings, conferences, hearings, and trials. And these limited interactions come together to form a reputation, one which a seasoned judge considers when evaluating a lawyer's argument or case-management requests. An attorney's reputation and interactions with the court have a great impact on whether a judge trusts a lawyer. Trust, or the absence of it, affects a judge's management and decision-making process in the case in which the lawyer is involved.

Not trustworthy? A court can hold the parties to a detailed plan for discovery to avoid one party taking advantage of another.

Deceitful? A court can discipline and sanction.

Honest and trustworthy? A court might well give you the benefit of the doubt.

A lawyer's reputation and conduct—and whether they can be trusted—is the filter through which the court evaluates if the lawyer's pleadings, presentations, representations, and arguments are credible. It is imperative that the attorney do everything in her power to establish that she can be trusted.

Consider the examples above. In the first case, the company lawyer took an aligned approach to his case. He wanted to achieve a specific result for his client, but also wanted to act reasonably and advance his client's interest in maintaining a good relationship with the union member. He did that by offering the union member the chance to express his complaints. Although the member ultimately acknowledged his conduct was wrong, the attorney took a different approach. He sought to repair the relationship by offering a resolution that accommodated both parties' interests, all without requiring a court order. His conduct aligned with his values—seek fair results, treat others with dignity, litigate efficiently, and resolve practically—and his actions in the courtroom that day advanced his reputation as an honorable attorney.

Different values were demonstrated by the conduct of the homeowner's lawyer in the insurance case. She illustrated contempt for the judicial system, her opposing party, its lawyers, and the presiding judge. She valued maximizing an award without regard to whether the amount sought was warranted. Her "ends justified the means" approach to the litigation frustrated the judicial process and the court's management of the case. And in the third example, to promote his own reputation with the court, a partner was willing to sacrifice the reputation of an associate working for him. That said, both of these lawyers could repair their reputation with the court. (No one is beyond reform.) How?

How a Court Sizes Up Counsel

Having presided over a couple of thousand cases and dealt with hundreds of attorneys, I've discovered six ways a lawyer can improve, and even repair, his or her relationship and reputation with the court:

1. Cultivate a good reputation among judges and the legal community.
2. Strive to plead and communicate with excellence, accuracy, and as simply as possible.
3. Comply with all applicable court rules.
4. Conduct yourself honestly and with candor.
5. Strive to conduct yourself with civility and dignity in court conferences, hearings, and trials.
6. Treat others the way you want to be treated.

Of course, the inverse is also true. To earn a poor reputation with the court, act in ways contrary to any of these six principles. Note that it only takes the violation of one of them to cast doubt upon your character. So, beware. The reputation you create will follow you, often longer than you'd like.

How do these six principles play out in building a reputation and relationship with the court? Let's look.

1. Cultivate a good relationship among judges and the legal community.

A number of months ago, I reviewed a list of all of the cases assigned to me when I was on the bench. As I reviewed it, I was surprised by how many of the lawyers in the cases I recalled by reputation. And that's when it struck me. Whenever I was assigned a new case, I first looked to see who represented the parties. The lawyers listed on the docket forecasted whether the case would be characterized by cooperation or conflict. I knew which lawyers might take advantage of counsel and the court and whether they could be trusted. These conclusions were based on the reputations of the lawyers who were involved. What's more, I used the reputation of the attorneys as a management tool. A lawyer's reputation had a meaningful effect on how I processed a case—that is, whether I managed it closely or gave the attorneys more liberty to work with less scrutiny. If I trusted them, I gave them freer rein.

And it's not just the presiding judges who form reputational opinions of attorneys. Other judges, law clerks, and courthouse staff offer insight into the trustworthiness of lawyers in a case. A staff member in my chambers once stopped by just before a hearing and shared that a certain lawyer—defense counsel in the case—was present and waiting in the courtroom. The attorney hadn't appeared in my court, but I had all the information I needed—the lawyer's name. His reputation was well established in the courthouse; other judges and staff members had described their experiences with him. Their feedback was consistent—be careful. My fellow judges and their staff members said you couldn't trust what he said, and that he'd make the hearing contentious and dispute every ruling. Everything will take longer than necessary or reasonable, they told me. With these consistent reports, how could I not be careful?

Good reputations are the ones most widely known. For example, I presided over a number of complicated securities-fraud class actions. These are intellectually difficult cases, involve significant claims of injury, and require close supervision. Despite all of that, these cases were among the most manageable of the cases over which I presided. That's because, as a rule, the lawyers were high-quality, trustworthy professionals. They explained complicated issues well and honestly, respected and accommodated the court, cooperated in discovery, and were fair. I came to know many of these lawyers by name, and when I saw them appear on my docket, I knew the case would proceed civilly and toward a just result.

2. Strive to plead and communicate with excellence, accuracy, and as simply as possible.

In a pleading, things catch a judge's attention. Whether the nature of the dispute supports the number of claims asserted tells a judge about a lawyer's litigation strategy. Did the lawyer take a "kitchen sink" claims approach to make the case seem more serious? Did he assert punitive damages, even though punitive damages weren't warranted in the type of action? These approaches suggest a lawyer may be intentionally overreaching or that the lawyer is not confident or experienced enough to eliminate claims that are not viable. They tell the court to be on guard.

Judges evaluate pleadings to see whether they are fairly and objectively asserted or whether they are inflammatory and perhaps used in a way to gain leverage or capture a little press coverage. In other words, judges examine pleadings and ask, "Does this pleading objectively, and in a simple, straightforward way, state the facts, or does it grandstand?" As no small aside, I had a simple test for determining whether a lawyer was grandstanding: I counted the number of adjectives and adverbs in the pleading. Overuse of adjectives and adverbs are classic devices to embellish weak claims and arguments. And this kind of pleading negatively impacts an attorney's reputation with the court. My cardinal rule is: facts and not your rhetoric are what persuade.

A lawyer's communications—usually correspondence and emails to opposing counsel—can also color a judge's opinion of counsel. Incivility in an attorney's communication tells a judge a lot about a lawyer's temperament and judgment, and they warn the judge to be leery of the lawyer who sends them.

3. Comply with all applicable court rules.

Court rules promote a level litigation playing field. While they may constrain lawyer conduct, the rules protect the court from unnecessary commitment of time and expense, and they serve the important purpose of ensuring both sides have the same opportunity to weigh in on an issue. A lawyer who complies with the rules builds a reputation for fairness, truthfulness, and justice. One who abuses or ignores the rules suggests a lawyer's objective is to win at all costs, even if the cost is justice and fairness. These reputations follow an attorney.

4. Conduct yourself honestly and with candor.

Lawyers are expected to be honest and transparent with the court. Put another way, attorneys owe the court a duty of candor. What is the best way to lose credibility and undermine your reputation with the court? Violate the duty of candor.

Criminal cases are where extraordinary candor happens. Here are two quick examples. I held a hearing on whether to grant a defendant's motion-to-dismiss indictment. As the hearing began, the government attorney asked to say something. She had done additional research before the hearing and discovered there was a case that contradicted an argument she had made in her brief. She said I had to follow the case because it was an opinion from our circuit and because of that the government was withdrawing the argument.

In another case, I considered a motion to suppress evidence obtained from a defendant's Blackberry device. We held a hearing on the motion at which the agent who interviewed the defendant testified that the defendant brought his Blackberry to the interview. When he was asked if he'd agree to allow the agent to review the defendant's emails, the defendant agreed and voluntarily entered his password so the emails could be accessed. I asked defense counsel if this changed his position, and the defense counsel said it did, acknowledging his client had agreed to the review.

Candor is important and if an attorney aligns to it, it can cement a reputation with a court.

Here's a story that makes the point. When I was the United States Attorney, I argued appellate cases before the Eleventh Circuit. Each of the appeals arose from cases that I tried before a jury. One of these appeals questioned the trial court's ruling on a defendant's motion to suppress evidence—a hidden firearm—discovered during a pat down. The search was in a high-crime area where police were patrolling, and this circumstance gives officers more liberty to protect their safety. The court denied the suppression motion and the defendant appealed his conviction and sentence.

I handled the argument at the circuit. I prepared hard, and we had a mock hearing where I answered questions that prosecutors in my office thought I might get asked at the oral argument. The practice was extremely helpful, and I was ready for my court appearance.

The argument went well, but there was one answer I gave in response to a question about facts in the record that I mulled over when I returned to my office. I thought there was a chance that I may not have answered the question as precisely as I wanted and decided to write a letter to the judges who heard my argument. I repeated the question asked and stated what I recalled as my answer. I told them that I had concluded my answer may not have been complete, and that I wanted to restate and elaborate on it in the letter. And I did. Satisfied that was the right thing to do, I had the letter hand-delivered to the court and to counsel for the defendant.

A few weeks later, I attended an annual luncheon for lawyers and federal judges. When I was walking to my assigned table, one of the appellate judges on the case called me over to her table. She'd received my letter and wanted to say that in all of the years she had served on the appeals court, she had never received a letter from a lawyer wanting to make sure what they argued was accurate. Because the letter was sent by a sitting United States Attorney, she thought it would make an impression on other prosecutors and emphasize a lawyer's obligation to the court.

The relationship with the court is among the most important for any litigator. A lawyer must gain the trust and respect of the court because doing so makes the lawyer's arguments and presentations to the court more trustworthy, credible, and persuasive. It may even influence the ultimate outcome of the case. But if the court believes a lawyer is not candid and is trying to manipulate the outcome, a court will consider the lawyer's position with caution.

5. Strive to conduct yourself with civility and dignity in court conferences, hearings, and trials.

In a hearing not long before I retired, a lawyer made an argument on behalf of her client. Her position was not well supported by cases in our circuit, and what's more, the argument was not otherwise persuasive. I ruled against her and proceeded to state the basis for my ruling so there would be a record on appeal if she chose to challenge it. As I was speaking, I heard a noise at the podium. I looked up just as she slammed her computer closed, haphazardly bundled her documents and removed them from the podium, and stomped back to counsel's table. There she stood with her arms folded, glaring at me while I made my findings. I finished and concluded the hearing. Her conduct was not new to me, though it was unexpected on that occasion. This act of defiance and disrespect for the court left a bold mark.

To be credible and trusted, a lawyer must be respectful and civil. This is especially true when responding to a question, comment, or ruling by the court. Comments and reactions must be reasonable and reasonably responsive to the issue discussed and to the questions asked. And when you lose a ruling, accept it. Theatrics are never appropriate or effective, even if you find them therapeutic or think they will impress a client. A lawyer has a duty to maintain the dignity of the judicial process, and that lack of dignity can have long-lasting and impactful results.

How a lawyer responds to questions asked by the court also can influence a court's impression of counsel. Did the lawyer provide the court the information necessary for the court to understand the status of a matter and the respective positions of the party? If the court asked counsel to move on from a point, did the lawyer comply? If the court offered suggestions, did the lawyer take them to heart or ignore them?

Early in my judicial career, I conducted a hearing on a motion for a temporary restraining order. The moving party alleged the former employee had started a competing business and that he was using the company's confidential information to do so. A court has considerable discretion to grant or deny a restraining order, and so it requires a lawyer to establish a great deal of credibility and trust with the court. I did not know the lawyer who filed the motion and did not know his firm.

The complaint and injunction motion asserted five claims for relief. The plaintiff's lawyer made the first presentation. He began by stating that after reviewing the claims asserted and thinking about the case overnight, he intended to move forward with only one claim. He said: "If my client is not entitled to relief on the first claim, we are not entitled to preliminary injunctive relief on the others." He made a reasonable, dispassionate argument that was respectful of his client's employee.

By narrowing his case to one claim, he focused the hearing and made the hearing more efficient. The facts he argued gave me a full picture of the dispute and allowed me to tailor an order that prohibited only certain conduct. His was a principled and honest approach, and it was good lawyering.

Lawyers must remember that the judge has a different perspective than the attorney. A lawyer focuses on his or her client's interests. The court's focus and interests are broader. There are times when I wished a lawyer could listen to how he or she sounded from my chair on the bench. Remember the example of the lawyer who slammed her computer shut? Maybe she wouldn't have done that if she saw what I saw—five high school students sitting in the back of the courtroom watching the proceeding as a class assignment. Perhaps she would have been more respectful of my ruling and the public forum if she understood her behavior affected her reputation with me and the students attending the proceeding.

6. Treat others the way you want to be treated.

Litigation is about human experience. It involves people and their conduct. And this includes the conduct that brought the parties to the courtroom in the first place, and the conduct of the lawyers and the parties in the courtroom once there.

When I first took the bench, I viewed a trial as a structured, orchestrated event which I managed. The longer I served, the more I recognized that each case was different, and to achieve a just result, each case had to be managed as a unique event, involving unique people with unique motivations. A wise lawyer told me early in my career that the lawyer's job in litigation is to find and understand the facts in a case and to take those unique facts and interpret them in a way that is most favorable to their client. The court's job is to assure a level playing field for the litigants so that each of the lawyers can advocate on his or her client's behalf, present the case efficiently, and assure that no party gets an unfair advantage. When all of this happens, a jury can render a fair decision. And that happens best when all parties involved treat each other the way they'd want to be treated themselves.

As I presided over cases, I was just as capable of making mistakes as were the lawyers involved. A respected lawyer whom I knew well did something that disrupted the orderly presentation of evidence in court, and my frustration with him got the better of me. Because of it, I made a statement about his conduct that was not appropriate. Fortunately, the jury was not present, but opposing counsel and the parties were.

At the end of the day, I sat in my office regretting what I had said. It was my responsibility to make amends. The next morning, I came in early and wrote an apology on one of my personal notecards. I put it in writing because I wanted it to have gravitas and because I wanted my expression of regret to be permanent. I had a member of my staff put the note on counsel's table so it would be there when he arrived that morning.

The next morning, I came into my office and found a note on my desk. In it, the lawyer wrote that both our jobs were hard but that we had too much history between us and that nothing could disrupt our relationship. (Incidentally, he said that my ruling had been correct, but he agreed I could have delivered it differently.) I'd treated him poorly, but by apologizing, I'd treated him the way I'd want to be treated had he offended me. It went a long way toward affirming our relationship and rebuilding trust.

The relationship between the lawyer and the court is critical in the pursuit of justice through the court system. Do your best to cultivate trust, and your practice will be more effective, less fraught with professional pitfalls, and more enjoyable. Lawyers and judges both should remember that. In all things we should act properly, fairly, and charitably. A little humility doesn't hurt either.

Building a reputation with the court is crucial. Equally important is building a reputation for mentoring and managing well. This kind of reputation doesn't happen overnight, and only the most aligned lawyers seek them out. How does the aligned lawyer mentor and manage? Let's look at that next.

Chapter 11

Managing and Mentoring

"Someone is sitting in the shade today because someone planted a tree a long time ago."
—*Warren Buffett, businessman,
investor, and philanthropist*

"Perfection is not attainable, but if we chase perfection, we can catch excellence."
—*Vince Lombardi, NFL coach*

Each year I was on the court I hired law clerks to help in my
work. And when one moved on, I posted the vacancy on a website judges use to solicit applications. The posting stated my hiring criteria, which included graduation in the top 10 percent of
the applicant's law school class, two to four years of practice experience, and law review membership in law school. I also noted
that the clerkship was eighteen months but could be extended.
Each time, I was flooded with applications, so many, in fact, that
I couldn't interview every qualified candidate who applied. I usually narrowed the field down to five or six and interviewed those
candidates with the help of my law clerks.

I had three principal goals in the interview process. First, I
wanted to determine if the applicant was called to public service,
which usually explained why they would leave practice for a clerk
position that paid a fraction of what they were earning. This was
a test of their commitment to our work. Second, I wanted to

know their approach to problem-solving and their reasoning skills. I needed to test their aptitude and academic qualifications for the work they'd be assigned. Finally, I wanted to determine their authenticity. We were a small, tight-knit work group. Each member of the chambers had to fit, and they had to be trusted. Authenticity and transparency evidenced these characteristics.

My questions were always open-ended because I wanted the applicant to do most of the talking. To investigate an applicant's purpose in seeking a chambers position, I'd ask what experience made them interested in public service work and where did public service work fit into their long-term professional plans. One applicant told me he needed a break from private practice and thought a clerkship would help his marketability. He had no core interest in a public service position, and that meant he was not aligned for the position. He was not a successful applicant.

To test reasoning and communication skills, I sometimes asked applicants what they thought was the greatest challenge to the independence of American courts. Other times, I asked the hardest legal issue they'd handled in their practice. Some of the off-the-cuff answers to these questions were remarkably insightful, cogently presented, and well reasoned. The applicants gave me a good sense of their analytical and communication ability, and most of the applicants I interviewed were up to the intellectual demands of the job.

Finally, I tested the applicant's authenticity, whether their behavior and character were the same with me as it was with the staff. I often asked what person or event had the greatest impact on their character. The responses to these questions indicated whether the candidate was authentic or not. I was often moved by the responses and the depth of self-reflection they demonstrated.

I didn't just judge their authenticity in chambers. I tested it before they ever set foot in my office. When an applicant was scheduled for an appointment, I'd ask my court reporter to sit in the reception area so he and my clerk—whose desk was in the front office—could talk with the potential clerk until I was available to meet. When my interview was over, I asked the court reporter and my clerk for their impressions of the candidate based on their conversation. These inputs were interesting, and on a couple of occasions, I declined to hire a lawyer because of the way they treated these members of my chambers' staff. I valued authenticity and character, and any potential clerk had to be aligned with that value, too. They had to treat everyone with respect and dignity if they were to fit into the team. After all, office relationships are strained if a clerk treats anyone on the staff as less important than others.

In my experience, hiring well enhances the chances that an applicant will align with the values required to be successful in the law clerk role. In my office, alignment to team values allowed any employee to have a fulfilling, satisfying, and productive stint. And though an employee and employer don't have to be aligned to all the same personal values, each must align to the shared values of the profession.

If the hiring process doesn't result in the hiring of an aligned employee, it quickly becomes obvious. That was particularly true in my job as a judge. The stress and demands of the legal profession—including judicial clerkships—are generally well known. So, I'd check the references of present and former employers and often independently called people with whom an applicant worked for their take on the applicant's qualifications to clerk. All of this information increases the chances of finding the right fit, but it does not perfectly protect against hiring mistakes. And hiring the wrong person has consequences.

The Consequences of a Mis-hire and the Importance of Mentoring

I recently visited a colleague who'd worked hard to hire bright, personable lawyers. I had met some of her hires, and they all seemed capable. But as we talked, she shared a problem. Over the past few weeks, she said, a young attorney had failed to show up for work on time, missed a number of deadlines, and produced poor work product that required hours of editing. The other lawyers in the office came to resent their colleague because they were required to take up the slack.

She had talked to the employee and tried her best to mentor her through the issues. She explained that tardiness and missing deadlines were not acceptable and that her work had to get better. It hadn't fixed the problem. Days later, she walked into the lawyer's unlit office an hour after the start of the workday and found her lying on the floor, earbuds in, listening to music. She asked her employee why she was lying on the floor. The young attorney sat up, looked at my friend, and explained that the work was much harder than she thought when she accepted the job and that listening to music helped alleviate stress. Soon after, she resigned.

My friend asked my thoughts, and I told her what she already knew. She'd been incredibly patient and had the right to confront her with her conduct. After all, the mis-hire had a significant impact on her staff, and she had tried to coax and coach the young woman into becoming a productive employee when that didn't work, it was right to pour her resources into finding a replacement and getting that replacement up to speed. What's more, she should look for someone who was coachable, someone who could be mentored.

Every good hiring decision is a collaboration between the employer and the employee. Both parties must ensure their values, ideals, and expectations align. If they do not, even the best hire can become dissatisfied. But how do you nurture alignment? Through mentoring.

I took my responsibility to mentor young lawyers seriously. When I joined the federal judiciary, I bucked the trend of hiring recent law school graduates, opting to hire only lawyers with practice experience. I wanted to give young lawyers the chance to step away from client-oriented advocacy and step into an environment in which we worked together on cases. I also wanted to offer a reprieve from the rancor that dominates private practice and allow them the space to rethink the trajectory of their career. I wanted to serve as a resource as they considered their career path.

Why did I value mentoring so much? Senior lawyers had mentored me when I was an associate, and I understood the role they'd played in forming my professional and personal values. I wanted to return that favor for the young lawyers who worked for me, but I did not want to limit it to them. In fact, for the past thirty years I've met with a large number of young lawyers who asked for a little career guidance. I've also met with more seasoned attorneys who've grown weary—sometimes disenchanted—with their work or their practice environment. I've poured into lawyers, young and experienced, because I want them to consider whether where they're working is where they're called to serve in our profession.

Active Managing Is Active Mentoring

The sad truth is that many attorneys haven't had great mentors. Lawyers get hired and they are put to work, often requiring them to fend for themselves. Career development is key to helping aligned hires stay aligned. Mentoring is a simple principle: active managing is active mentoring.

Whether as a partner, agency head, or a judge, I always tried to manage lawyers in a way that gave them a degree of control over their work while still providing input and advice. I allowed them to take the reins on cases, to do their own research and form their own opinions. When needed, I stepped in and gave pointers about how to approach a case or helped them to interpret facts. We talked about their families, friends, and outside interests and the importance of maintaining each of these. I was not a passive manager, as many lawyers are these days. I actively invested in the development of the lawyers who worked with me because that was a key responsibility I had as a leader, and so I mentored throughout the day.

Active management does not mean giving your employees the answers. As a judge, I believed I'd get the very best thinking from my clerks if they did not know my thoughts on a particular case. After reviewing the arguments—whether in a brief or at a hearing—I tasked my clerks with researching and reaching a reasoned and correct decision. To learn, they had to risk being wrong. Sometimes they struggled in the process, but I always got superior work from them by entrusting them to use their skills, even if I didn't agree with their conclusions. And when I disagreed, I always explained why. Sometimes, my years of experience simply gave me a different perspective of the facts and a deeper understanding of the applicable law. Sometimes, I simply disagreed with an interpretation. But these moments of critical feedback and disagreement created real learning opportunities for those clerks, strengthened their analytical skills, and made me think about whether my conclusion was correct. And as I discovered, lawyers thrive in environments where their work is critiqued by a lawyer invested in their development and success.

I also debriefed my law clerks about hearings and trials. We discussed lawyer presentations, witness testimony, how lawyers handled issues arising at trial, how we'd managed the litigation process, and how they responded to the court's directives. These discussions usually occurred at the end of the day when we were winding down and we could more leisurely discuss our profession using real-time examples.

Of course, I didn't adopt this sort of management style when I became a judge. I'd offered it when I was in private practice and when I was the United States Attorney. As United States Attorney, I often met with prosecutors about the progress of their cases. There, we kicked around investigation strategies and how to follow up on leads. I often asked them to outline the evidence they'd developed and identify what more we needed to prove a crime. I'd slipped into the back of the courtroom when cases were tried and watched examinations or arguments. Often, I'd stop by the lawyer's office at the end of the day to discuss the lawyer's courtroom performance.

Over the years, I've come to call these day-by-day interactions "active mentoring." It was part of my ongoing process of helping younger lawyers develop good judgment, trial prowess, professional conduct, and effective trial-management skills in the context of the work they were doing. I was committed to the development of those coming behind me because this kind of active mentoring is every lawyer's obligation, one that is today too often neglected.

Lawyer Development—Mentoring by Doing

I didn't just manage and mentor attorneys at the United States Attorney's office, I also led and mentored by example by prosecuting difficult cases. Among them was a complicated fraud scheme in which a defendant entered into a conspiracy to dupe a paper-manufacturing company by creating fake invoices for timber that was never delivered. The amount of the fraud was in the neighborhood of $7 million dollars. I tried the case with a very able AUSA. We shared the responsibility for questioning witnesses, making legal arguments, and introducing evidence. I gave the opening statement and we split the closing. During my portion of the closing argument, I glanced at the public seating area and was surprised to see a number of lawyers from our office watching. They were learning by observing and showing their support for our work on the case. I think some of them wondered if I really was able, like them, to try a case.

The jury deliberated less than an hour before returning a guilty verdict. My co-counsel and I returned to the office to debrief the case. Once there, a number of people who watched the closing stopped in. They hadn't come simply to congratulate us. They asked about our presentation and how I decided on the structure of it. Some noted that I hadn't simply pawned the case off on my cocounsel but had divided trial responsibilities equally, treating her as an equal member of the team. I found out later that some in the office were surprised that I would entrust management of the office I lead to someone else while I prepared and tried the case.

Weeks later, I began hearing what was being said behind closed doors. The lawyers I supervised were impressed that I'd actually tried a case to a jury, and in doing so, had run the risk of damage to my credibility if I lost. As I caught wind of these private conversations, and as more attorneys began asking me about their own cases, I was convinced: mentors lead by doing.

Those entering the practice of law today yearn for community and purpose. They want to be a member of a team, and they want to know how their work fits into the bigger picture. They want to learn the nuts and bolts of practice—how to draft and respond to discovery, take depositions, or introduce evidence at trial—but they also want the satisfaction of knowing how all the pieces, including the ones they produced, work to produce results. This kind of understanding comes only by working alongside and learning from more seasoned attorneys. This sort of active mentorship will never happen unless there is a culture of collaboration and cooperation.

I learned firsthand how to create a collaboration and cooperation culture when I joined the Whitewater Independent Counsel's office in Little Rock in the mid-90s. Bob Fiske was the independent counsel, and he wanted to hire a staff from across the country. I was one of Bob's early hires, and so I had the opportunity to watch him build his team from the ground up. Once assembled, I noticed how he nurtured the group through his management style. Cooperation and coordination were important to the investigation, he said, and synergistic thinking was invaluable. So, Bob called meetings regularly to share progress in the investigation and to examine investigation strategies together.

Bob also avoided unnecessary hierarchy. He didn't call people down to his office to meet. He came to yours. He encouraged and participated in social events. He gathered us for lunches. He knew the names of the spouses and children of team members. We knew what everyone was doing and the progress each of us was making. Young lawyers often made invaluable suggestions at our meetings, and they contributed more because they knew the whole of our work and how each facet of the investigation was related. And though we didn't operate under the tyranny of the billable hour, I knew Bob hadn't let billable-hour concerns dictate how he worked with others when he was in private practice. I had it on good authority that he often took time out of his day to work with younger lawyers, and he took this same approach at the independent counsel's office.

Effective mentoring is a day-to-day activity involving real matters and real clients. It requires active management and leading by example, which senior lawyers achieve by investing in the development of younger ones as they work together on a matter. This kind of mentoring is the most effective and cost efficient. A firm may also want to consider a program pairing younger lawyers with experienced attorneys who mentor a young lawyer assigned to them. But I caution that this kind of program might not have the scope of impact a firm seeks and can send a message to lawyers that mentoring is an after-hours, or when-time-permits, activity. Also, some senior lawyers are not as effective in guiding lawyers in a structured mentoring program, and pairings are not always natural ones. Like most tasks at a firm, responsibility ought to be assigned to those most qualified and experienced to perform them. The bottom line is that today, young lawyers want a firm that is invested in their career development, and all options should be explored.

But How Do We Charge for Mentoring?

I remember a partner in a meeting once say that we pay lawyers to produce, not learn. "We can't bill for learning," he said in jest, but behind every joke is an underlying truth. Assigning and billing for tasks certainly makes practical sense, but how can you induce older lawyers to participate in mentorship programs? And how can you incentivize junior lawyers to sit in on client meetings, even if they don't bill for it, so they can see how their legal research shapes the counsel given? The truth is, current billing practices often discourage mentoring, active or otherwise, and it is a barrier to equipping the practitioners of the future, which is to say nothing of building collegiality between seasoned attorneys and the younger lawyers they work with.

The billable hour is the driver for so much of law practice. The number of hours billed and the income those hours represent affects the compensation a lawyer receives, their advancement opportunities, the assignments they get, their reputation in a firm, and even the amount of time they spend with their families. Some law firms give summaries of billable time, which might include each lawyer's billable and nonbillable time, the average billable and nonbillable hours for members on their team, and the average billable time for each member of the firm. This allows a lawyer to see how they stack up against the billable-hour totals of others. And competitive as they are, most lawyers are seldom satisfied with being average, and so they push harder, bill more. And if a firm can get everyone to meet or exceed the average billable hours, the average will naturally increase, requiring lawyers to work harder and longer.

The competitive desire to maximize billable hours is a significant disincentive to helping others, can create an insurmountable barrier to mentoring, and robs lawyers of time for outside interests and family. It strains lawyers' relationships. What incentives exist for partners and associates who may not be able to bill for the mentoring process? Few to none. Lawyers and their firms need to think differently and innovatively about how to encourage lawyer interactions and mentoring in a billable-hour world.

If collegiality and work-product excellence are values of the firm, then mentoring must not just be enabled, but encouraged. Make it permissible for junior lawyers to ask for help across teams so they can get the training they need. Consider granting financial rewards for those who mentor or assist junior attorneys instead of reducing their income or degrading their stature. Treat mentoring time as valuable as billable time, report it as so, and see what happens.

No matter how much you mentor, there may come a time when a lawyer can't seem to align themselves to the firm or the practice of law. What can these lawyers do to make their legal and personal life better? They may need to pivot, a seemingly risky decision. But as we'll see, a good pivot (both in position and priorities) might be just the thing to bring about true job satisfaction in a legal career.

Chapter 12

Priorities and Pivots

"We had more in common than I thought we did.
You were my priority. You were your priority."
—*Kate McGahan, writer and social worker*

"School plays were invented partly to give parents an
easy opportunity to demonstrate their priorities."
—*Calvin Trillin, journalist and writer*

In 1999, things were going well in my practice. I had interesting,
complex, fee-generating cases and was proving to be successful
in generating new work. I was in the litigation fast lane, one that
led to partnership advancement and recognition in my firm and
community. But then one day, things at home began to fall
apart.

I'd like to say the collapse was unexpected. It would be more
honest to say I ignored signs forecasting the problem, because
ignoring them was both convenient and allowed me to focus on
my practice. The more I thought about my career, the more I
recognized how I contributed to a general deterioration of my
marriage and my estrangement with my children. I hadn't given
my family the priority it deserved. And though I would have told
you I was actively engaged in my sons' lives, I didn't attend their
school plays and events. Family activities were nowhere to be
found on my calendar.

You might be asking what the calendar has to do with it, but bear with me. For years, I used a month-at-a-glance calendar to keep my schedule. I liked the format because a quick review of a month gave me an immediate sense of how scheduled I was and where I had capacity to pencil in new events. At the end of each year, I stashed my completed calendar in a filing-cabinet drawer, and by 2000 I had almost twenty years of month-at-a-glance books.

With years of calendar data at my fingertips, I decided to look at my schedule for the months leading up to our family crisis and examine the pace of my life. So, I pulled my calendars for 1997 and 1998, and as I thumbed through them and my 1999 calendar, I was surprised by how many entries I had for each month. I'd calendared each of my cases and the flow of activities on them. There were planned and unplanned legal events, internal firm meetings and responsibilities, and business-generating appointments. I'd also recorded the time I'd committed to non-profit boards, church committee meetings, practice development dinners, and professional outings. My calendar included the usual panoply of things you'd expect of a partner in a busy litigation practice at a big firm, and reviewing those calendars brought back the stress and the anxiety that accompanied that season.

During my entry-by-entry review, I looked for activities at my sons' school, sporting events, Scouting activities, and occasions alone with my wife. There was a paucity of entries for personal events. I knew there had to be more than those I recorded, and so I looked at the entries again, trying to find the personal activities I knew I'd attended. They weren't on my calendar. As I tried to reconstruct events, I realized that time had slipped by faster than I remembered, and things I thought had happened in the years I reviewed had actually occurred well before, sometimes by a couple of years. What's more, for the personal events that were recorded (and for some I hadn't written down), I recalled that I too often hadn't arrived on time because of work obligations. I even remembered feeling anxious at the kids' events I attended because I was distracted by some client or firm responsibility. After spending several hours reviewing these calendar years, I found I was not as present as often as I remembered, and when I was actually there, I wasn't mentally or emotionally present at all. No wonder I felt estranged from my family.

Why were there so few personal events on my calendar? I eventually admitted that my personal obligations were not important enough to make it to my calendar because my priority was to meet client demands and take on other career-enhancing activities. While I told plenty of people that I valued my relationship with my wife and sons, my conduct certainly was not aligned with the "priority" I touted. How did I correct this? One conversation helped me start.

The Equal Dignity Rule

Larry Thompson is a dear friend and someone who has spoken into my life for nearly thirty years. We were partners at King & Spalding, and one evening, while working on a case together, I stopped by his office so we could call a lawyer in California about an issue important to our client. We discussed the matter, but Larry's plan did not include calling the California attorney that day. I argued that it was three hours earlier in California and that the lawyer we needed to call might still be at work. I suggested that calling the attorney might earn some points with him, but Larry doubted it. And then he said this: "I've always admired how hard you work on cases and how responsive you are to clients and others. You are always available, and people know that about you. I'm just not sure that is best for your work or for you."

I was dumbstruck, and I stood staring at him as the silence hung. Hard work and responsiveness weren't best for my work or for me? Wasn't that the cornerstone of good lawyering?

He continued: "I've found that letting things settle has a couple of benefits. Just because something is urgent to someone else doesn't mean it's *actually* urgent. You may find by letting some time pass a response is not needed at all because the situation resolves itself."

That made some sense, and I believed it was true.

Larry went on: "Not always being available can make you more valuable. If someone wants to meet and you cannot jump to it, the person calling will assume others have your time. Meeting with you is valuable to them, it is why they called. So, they'll be much more flexible in scheduling if they know they have to compete with others for your time."

Larry wrapped up the conversation by saying that not always responding to the demands of others gives a lawyer more discretion in allocating their time. It allows you to set your priorities and organize your time around what is most important. Larry's insight helped me understand my calendar problem. I was populating my calendar with client and professional obligations, leaving little capacity to schedule anything else. I even declined to add personal events to my calendar because I wanted unscheduled time to add new work activity. Larry's comments made me face the hard truth: I devoted every spare minute of my most valuable resource—time—to my clients, reserving none for my family. Why? Because I wasn't assigning the proper value to my time, and I wasn't showing my wife and children the dignity they deserved by reserving time for them.

My love for my family was a very real value. Still, I failed to align my conduct to it. But what would happen—what would my calendar and life look like—if I gave important personal activities "equal dignity" with work obligations? The deterioration of my relationship with my family convinced me I had to do something different, and I thought a different approach to calendaring events might help.

I plan almost everything, so I decided on a two-step approach. First, I made a personal commitment to reduce my billable hours by 10 percent and reallocate that time to repairing my family relationships. Second, every meaningful activity with my family was placed on my calendar, and I committed to not substituting some work obligation for a personal one.

My plan was tested quickly. I received a call from a client I had represented for years. He said he needed to meet midmorning on the following day to discuss an issue. I looked at my calendar and found I was scheduled to attend "Dad's Day" at my son's school during the time my client suggested for the meeting. I admit I was reluctant to turn down the client request, but I told him I had an appointment. I offered alternative times, told him I could carve out an hour late in the afternoon or early evening, and that I could meet anytime the following day. Those times didn't work for him. He suggested we meet on Thursday when I was available, and that's when it became apparent. The issue he wanted to talk about wasn't a drop-everything-and-respond issue. It could wait a couple of days, and the client wasn't upset by the delay.

Admittedly, I didn't explain my scheduling conflict, and he didn't ask. But as I've continued to turn down work-related meetings when they conflicted with scheduled family events, I began explaining to my clients my policy regarding calendaring time with my family. My clients rarely took issue with my personal commitments, and, in fact, I've found over the years that people respect my commitment to personal priorities. What's more, this practice has opened up conversations about our families and personal lives, allowing for deeper personal connection with others. And by aligning my calendar with my core values, I've recaptured my time and sent this clear message to my family: *You are worthy of as much dignity as my work.*

But what about lawyers with whom and against whom I litigated? Do they understand when I can't tend to a matter because of a family event? Of course, they do. In fact, years ago, I found myself speaking on the phone with a lawyer I had litigated with and against. I knew her well. We attended the same church, and I knew she struggled to balance her work with time with her young children. She called to get on my calendar on a Friday, a day I had promised to take off to go camping with my son's Scout troop. I told her I was not available, and she responded with deep understanding: "What you are doing is more important than our meeting. How do you look on Monday?" Monday worked fine.

I hope my decision left a mark. I hope it influenced her to examine her own calendar and align her actions accordingly. What's more, I hope she teaches her partners and associates how to align their personal values with their client demands. If she does, I believe her work will be more fulfilling and satisfying. How do I know? Because I've lived it.

Understanding the Time Quadrants: Applying Them to a Balanced Life

Stephen Covey, A. Roger Merrill, and Rebecca R. Merrill wrote a management book entitled *First Things First.*[1] The book was transformative, and it gave me a structure to evaluate how to manage time, one I've used to manage my work and personal commitments. In the book, the authors argue that life activities fall within the following four quadrants:

[1] Stephen Covey, A. Robert Merrill, and Rebecca R. Merrill, *First Things First: To Live, To Love to Leave a Legacy* (New York: Simon and Schuster, 1994) (ISBN 0-684-80203-1). This work provides invaluable information to help manage personal and professional lives.

I. Important/ Urgent	II. Important/ Not Urgent
III. Not Important/ Urgent	IV. Not Important/ Not Urgent

Quadrant I events—important and urgent—don't occur often, but when they do, they are obvious. It might be an immediate health issue, a child who's in danger, or an unexpected event that threatens the viability of a business. When these things happen, you drop everything and tend to them. No questions asked. Apologize after the fact if needed.

Quadrant IV—unimportant and not urgent—are the activities of an ordinary day, and they are similarly obvious. Watching TV and surfing the internet are a couple of the activities in Quadrant IV. We do not have a problem recognizing and prioritizing Quadrant I and Quadrant IV activities. These are the things that end up taking care of themselves. After all, if it's important and urgent, you'll drop everything to get to it. If it's unimportant and not urgent, you can skip it without consequence. Where I, and most people, struggle is in recognizing and prioritizing activities in Quadrants II and III.

Items in Quadrant II (important and not urgent) and Quadrant III (not important and urgent) compete for our time. It is our quadrant battleground. In my own legal practice, I struggled to devote time to Quadrant II. Family, friends, church, and fitness were important but not urgent, and so I always rationalized that I'd find time to squeeze them into my busy work schedule. Those items gave way to client and work demands in Quadrant III. They were often (maybe usually) not important, but because they were part of my career duties, they seemed urgent, or a client made them seem so. Decisions to be available to clients for their work, admittedly not important but deemed urgent, robbed me of the time for activities and opportunities in Quadrant II and threw me out of alignment.

The easiest examples of important, albeit not urgent, Quadrant II activities involve family relationships. To anyone in a demanding career, this shouldn't come as any surprise. It's easy for high-performing, ambitious professionals to pay less attention to family activities and concerns because professional and personal recognition seem more important and more measurable. Professional activities also seem to offer greater, more tangible rewards. I know now that this is not the case. Attending to the nonurgent, important things in life—particularly friends, faith, and family—has a direct impact on professional success. The emotional stability provided by family is what promoted my professional accomplishments. Tension at home has a real impact on concentration at work, relationships with work colleagues, and productivity. I've seen lawyers struggle through divorces, substance abuse issues with children, and disciplinary problems with their children at school, all of which affected their work. I've also seen the stability of a good marriage, well-grounded children, and close relationships with friends and colleagues. In fact, when my family has felt loved and supported, they have been the biggest champions of my work.

I would never had joined the independent counsel's staff in Arkansas during the investigation of President and Mrs. Clinton had it not been for my wife, Betsy. After I was asked to join the investigation, I discovered I had to withdraw from my partnership and cash out of its retirement system. There was risk associated with leaving a prominent law firm and reducing my income by 80 percent. There was uncertainty of my marketability when the investigation concluded, and I wondered whether I'd be able to make up lost income. I had doubts about whether it made financial or professional sense to take the position. It was hard to evaluate the uncertainly of the future.

As I struggled with all of these concerns, Betsy weighed in. We were sitting in our family room on a Saturday morning, and she said she wanted to talk out the decision. She and the kids were all in if I wanted to leave my firm and live in Arkansas, where the investigation was headquartered. We could downsize our life financially, sell the house if we had to, and adjust our lives to make the most of life in a different place. "I know you're worried about the risk of going," she said, "but I also know you think the work is important. I don't know anyone better qualified or with more integrity than you, and for that reason you should go."

That final encouragement was what I needed, and it changed the trajectory of my life. It let me know that my family was behind me and that they trusted me to make the right decision. And in this way, the thing that was most important in my life—my wife and children—helped me tackle an assignment that was less important but most certainly urgent.

The Covey quadrants are a helpful tool to help me balance my time and adjust my calendar. Over the years, they've helped me ensure I'm prioritizing properly and living aligned with my professional and personal values. And as I've demonstrated throughout this book, it is this kind of aligned living that leads to fulfillment.

The Call to Align

Ralph (different from the Ralph who helped me understand why retiring a mortgage is a sound idea) and I were contemporaries at King & Spalding. We both were partners on the litigation team, and, for a while, Ralph served as our team leader. He represented good clients and he tried complex commercial cases. I envied Ralph, a hard-working attorney who was guided by strongly held beliefs and values, and who never seemed to veer off course. He was aligned with what he believed, and it showed in his daily routine.

I worked long hours at my firm, and while I sat at my desk hammering out some pleading at the dinner hour, Ralph was busy straightening up his desk to go home. Ralph left for dinner with his family almost every night, but now I know it was because he knew what was important, even if not urgent, and he committed time to those things I often ignored. He prioritized his family time and other commitments important to him personally. This is not to say Ralph wasn't committed to excellence in representing his clients. He was. So, during office hours, he was totally focused at work and was unequaled in the efficient use of his time because he was motivated by his unequaled devotion to his family. If he hadn't finished his work for the day, he'd find time later that didn't interfere with the time he reserved for his family.

But he didn't just prioritize time for his family relationships. Ralph found time to serve at his church, something that played an important role in his life. He served on boards because he thought board leadership was important. He made time for the things that improved the quality of his life, knowing that those things would actually bring him more satisfaction. And the more satisfied he was, the better off he knew he'd be.

Ralph was a valued partner at our firm, and he was respected for his balance because it helped him bond with colleagues and clients. And then one day, while still relatively young, he announced he was leaving the firm to return to his home state of North Carolina. He'd accepted a role as general counsel at a chain of retail stores, and though this was an unusual move for a young and up-and-coming, big-law equity partner, I knew he'd made the right decision. I knew his connection to North Carolina, and the pull of his family there was strong. He would be returning to the place where his values had been formed. I knew that he was leaving behind a significant potential for income and membership in a firm that was positioned to be one of the great firms in the country. Ralph, though, was drawn by other things, and he could best align his career with his values by moving home. And in the long run, it served to enhance his reputation. I still consider Ralph one of the most disciplined and productive lawyers I've known, but even more, I consider him one of the most aligned.

Aligning is not for the faint of heart, and the process takes time, hard work, and often risk and sacrifice. It begins with a high degree of introspection. You must examine your professional and personal values and ask whether you agree with the shared values of our profession and your firm or organization. If your professional values are different than the values of others, why is that? Finally, ask what you might need in your professional and personal life to be fulfilled?

How we spend our time shows whether we are in or out of alignment with our core values. Do we leave early from work to attend our daughter's play, or do we ignore the clock and keep our head down to work on finishing a memo that could be completed tomorrow morning by coming in early? Do we schedule a cup of coffee with a young associate to help her work through a conflict with a partner rather than schedule a business phone call that can be conducted later? Do we seek appointment to a nonprofit board whose work we admire, knowing it may result in having to decline a new matter due to time constraints? Each of these decisions affects personal alignment, but these decisions also send an important message to other lawyers, especially new ones. It isn't always easy to align or to sustain alignment once obtained. But it is worth the commitment. Let me help by giving you a little perspective.

Chapter 13

Perspectives on Alignment

"We don't drift in good directions. We discipline and prioritize ourselves there."

—*Andy Stanley, writer and pastor*

"How can I get your job?"

He was a young associate at a respected law firm in town, and this was the first question he asked as he sat in my chambers. Truth be told, the question wasn't surprising. He wasn't the first lawyer to ask me about the path to becoming a judge, so his limited focus on career trajectory wasn't new to me. But I needed more information about his background before I responded to his question, assuming that was the question he really wanted answered.

I asked about his family, where he grew up, where he went to college, what he majored in and why, the work activities he liked, and his outside interests. I asked about his prior work experience and the reasons for his change of employers. He answered all of my questions, and having the background information I wanted, I asked, "Why did you go to law school?" This was always my culminating question when talking to those young lawyers who wanted to be judges, and the answers shared varied wildly. And it was this question that typically showed me they cared less about being a judge and more about determining where they fit in the legal profession.

There were attorneys who told me they applied to law school because they wanted to do some sort of graduate work, and law school seemed challenging and practical. A few had worked in other fields after college, and, dissatisfied with the career path, had decided to go back to school. Two separate lawyers said they were pushed toward law school by their peers. A couple told me they'd chosen law school because people they knew had commented on their argument skills. When I asked one lawyer what drew him, he looked at me and said, "I have no idea."

There were a small number of people who had thought long and hard about attending law school. They'd counted the cost. Some had parents or relatives who practiced law, and though they got a firsthand glance into what the law practice required— the long hours, the stress and anxiety—these attorneys also knew that the satisfaction of helping others outweighed the burdens of practice. Some didn't have relatives in the profession, but they had met with lawyers to talk about the profession before entering the field. They'd asked questions about the compensation and the different areas of practice available to lawyers. They had a good sense of what lawyers did and the rewards of the work. They'd chosen to attend law school because the profession seemed like the right career path.

In listening to all these stories, I discovered there is a strong correlation between the reason someone enters law and their satisfaction in practice. Those who had a strong desire to serve others, liked intellectual rigor and challenges, and who understood the stresses and tedium of practice before entering law school were much more satisfied. Those who had meandered into the profession were less satisfied and likely not the best fit for the bench.

The fellow sitting in my office on that particular day wasn't looking to serve the community as a judge. He was looking for a route to escape from where he was—a practice he found a burden. The truth is, many of my "how do you become a judge" conversations are like that. The question is often posed by lawyers who want to find the satisfaction in work they sought when they entered law school. But some were out of alignment with law practice from the beginning.

Every lawyer must find their place in our profession. Ideally, this fit inquiry begins before you are awarded your law degree. Regrettably, from my conversations with those new to the profession, law school career-placement offices don't help much with fit evaluations. But even if you didn't enter into an alignment analysis before you entered the practice of law, it's never too late to begin.

Partial Alignment Isn't Perfect Alignment

Over my forty years of listening to lawyers' stories, I found there are many who don't get much pleasure from the practice of law. These lawyers still tend to be ethical, fair, and civil. They align with many of the professional values lawyers share, while their personal values lean toward economic and material security. Many measure their success by their income. Most acknowledge they might value stature and financial stability more than the profession itself and the work they do each day. And this focus on security and identity affects how they practice and their job satisfaction. But they are content to remain practitioners, even if not truly fulfilled by their work.

On a long drive to meet with a client, I had a conversation with one such lawyer. He spoke a lot about his practice, client development, and his progression to senior partner at his firm. I asked him to tell me his most important priorities in life. He thought for a couple of minutes and then said his first priority was his health, because he needed to be healthy to sustain his ability to work to generate income. His second priority, he said, was his family. He worked to provide a certain kind of lifestyle for them. His third priority was his faith, and he believed if he was financially stable, and his family satisfied and happy, then he'd be in the best position to help his church. When he'd finished outlining his priorities, he said, "I never realized how my priorities all interrelate."

As I considered his comments, I supposed he lived his values. Older than I was, he was fit and had a disciplined daily exercise regimen. His lifestyle was well established. He owned a home in a neighborhood where many of the city's corporate leaders lived, and he was a member of social organizations with prominent city citizens. His family had plenty of money to do the things they wanted to do. And, as a leader in his church, he was able to influence and help fund the church's ministries. His conduct aligned with his values, and he was a terrific man, but he didn't get up each morning knowing he was going to do work he loved. For him, that didn't matter as much.

This might be okay for my friend, but it's not how I, and many of the other lawyers I've talked with over the years, want to be aligned. Most of us want to be aligned to all parts of the profession, including to understand and serve the needs and desires of our clients, to serve the community and maintain the quality and availability of legal services to those who need them, and to achieve fair, just results for fair compensation. To be clear, alignment does not mean you cannot have significant material success. It only means that financial success is the by-product of having values that are best aligned to the values of being an attorney, values such as intellectual curiosity, hard work, judgment, passion for the law, and compassion for people. Lawyers who hold these core values will find more meaning and fulfillment in their careers, and the natural result may be increased financial stability.

Proper Alignment Takes a
Constant Inventory of Values

Values and alignment are not static. You may join a firm or company based on certain values you embraced early in your career. But then you marry, or have children, or someone in your family gets ill, or you connect with a population that needs help, and your values change. You might want to spend more time with your family or in your community. You might decide to fight for the rights of others. You might want to get more involved in policy or management issues where you work. You might want to offer the next part of your career to public service. There may be times when you find you're not aligned with your current position. When that happens, you might need to make an adjustment.

Early in my career, my priorities shifted. I wanted more value-oriented work, wanted to be more available to my wife and sons, and to be more involved in my community. I also wanted to practice in a different area of law, litigating hard, challenging cases that made a difference. Wanting advice, I talked about my shift with a friend, and he suggested I talk with an executive coach he knew. I scheduled the meeting, and when the day came, I described to the coach why I thought I needed to make a change. She listened and repeated the things I'd found unsettling at work. She suggested that many professionals want to escape their jobs not because they are dissatisfied with the work, but because of their dissatisfaction with the environment in which they worked. She then reminded me that I had a strong practice and presence in the community and that I liked the litigation work I was doing. She understood that I didn't like the subject matter but said I should be reluctant to discard the platform I'd earned. That's when she issued some of the wisest counsel I've ever received.

"It seldom makes sense to leave without first exploring if you can change your practice and the environment where you are," she said. "There may be intangible and tangible costs to make a change within your firm, but the cost may be materially more if you move to practice somewhere else, and you risk not finding what you want." Essential to her advice was a core message: if I could align my values and work with the values and work of another department within the firm, I'd be better off in the long run. It was sage advice I hadn't expected. So, I changed my practice and joined a team more aligned with my values and work interests. She was right. I suffered a little financial bump, but the long-term reward was significant. Ultimately, I discovered it is easier to be satisfied, productive, and financially content when your career is aligned with what is personally and professionally important to you. And from time to time, you may need to make an alignment adjustment.

A Word for Young Lawyers

When I was on the board of the Atlanta Track Club, we evaluated the demographics of our membership in anticipation of a new-member campaign. The ATC had pivoted from an event-driven organization to one whose mission was to improve health and fitness in Atlanta through running and walking. The data we collected showed that our members were predominantly middle-aged, and we needed to attract young people if the ATC was to continue to have the resources to support our community. Our research also showed that organizations addressing a significant social issue and which created a sense of community were most likely to attract millennials. ATC offered both of these—social purpose and community—and our membership fee was low. Shouldn't our organization interest young people? If so, why was our sign-up low?

I knew there was lots of buzz about cycling studios in Atlanta, and different companies were opening them across the city. These studios had become an exercise haven for millennials.

So, I decided to start attending one to see for myself what the attraction was and to see how it compared to our offerings. The experience was interesting. Young people mainly showed up. They didn't talk much to each other and they pedaled in the dark, following directives shouted at them by the instructor, who was spinning under a spotlight. I attended for a few weeks, enjoying the class but not fully understanding the millennial draw. I thought the track club offered more.

After class one day, I finally asked a young woman why she came to the class. She said she liked to exercise, but she came to this studio because it was the closest exercise place near where she worked. She then volunteered, "But that's no longer the case."

"Why?" I asked.

She came to Atlanta to work at a public relations firm, she told me. She had been there about a year and decided the firm should consider some changes that would improve the work environment for employees. She'd made some suggestion about how work should be assigned, and those suggestions weren't well received. So, she quit, stating she wasn't going to work where she was not respected and appreciated.

I left the conversation bewildered. I knew the public relations firm she left. It was large and respected. I suspected they were selective in their hiring process, extending offers to only the most qualified candidates. And her decision—to leave because her suggestions about business operations were not adopted— seemed shortsighted. In fact, her decision failed to show any appreciation for the employment opportunity at a firm that had worked awfully hard to create a successful and revered business. She seemed to lack any sense of gratitude for the career opportunity and the good salary that came with it. I wanted to talk with her about the value of gratitude and about being realistic about her place in the organization, but I didn't. I simply wished her a good morning and returned to my office.

I considered this young woman's comments in light of my own career. I remembered sitting in law school orientation before classes started. The students around me had graduated from some of the best colleges and universities in the country. Their undergraduate grades were stellar, as were their law school entrance scores. It became apparent that my college achievements did not guarantee my success in law school. I'd have to compete with the best students from some of the best colleges and universities around the country. I'd have to prove myself all over again. I was up for the challenge, grateful for the opportunity to study law. I worked hard and did well.

I graduated, served my active-duty air force obligation, and then was offered a job at King & Spalding, an envied firm that hired top talent. On my first day, I looked around at the associates on my team and realized I again had to distinguish myself, this time from the best and most talented young lawyers from the top law schools in the country. We all had similar credentials. Still, there were differences among us.

Some produced better written work product. Some communicated with outsiders better than others, some actively sought additional duties and case assignments, and others connected with organizations in the community and sought leadership positions in them. Some gossiped; some didn't. Some were awkward in social settings; some were not. There was a whole panoply of skills, weaknesses, and idiosyncrasies among those starting out at the firm. I certainly had my own.

As I continued into my first year, I took note. Some associates distinguished themselves. They were seen as stronger lawyers with partner potential. Others were good lawyers and fine people, but it became clear they didn't have all the skill sets or the drive needed to be elected as owners of the firm.

I realized I was in a winnowing process and I didn't want to be winnowed out. My commitment was to do my best, work harder than others, listen to feedback I received, and improve my practice skills. I didn't resent the process. I believed rewards would come from hard work, commitment, and excellence, and I dedicated myself to those principles.

There wasn't any coddling at the firm, but it was never unkind. The feedback from the partners was realistic and sometimes more honest that I liked. One partner liked that I had discipline and a drive to succeed, and he characterized my work this way: "When you're told to take the mountain you don't look for the easiest switchback. You forge straight to the top." He told me my drive was strong and that it was one of my most valuable attributes. But then he offered this constructive criticism: "When you forge ahead on the hardest route, you ignore that those working with you may not have the ability to keep up. Some have said you think you are better than others. But the truth is, you'll always need the help to get to the top. Leadership is important here. You've got to make sure you help people take the summit with you even if they don't have the drive or stamina that you have." The message was delivered kindly, but it was demoralizing. The practice of law required skills different and more refined than the skills required to study law. It was a valuable insight, although it became clear that simply having a strong work ethic and commitment to the work did not necessarily entitle me to make partner. Excellence in the practice of law, I found, included honing the ability to manage people and earn respect. Though this message was tough to hear, it was crucial. It allowed me the opportunity to compete (even against myself) to have a chance to advance. It also led me to understand and align my behavior with the values of the firm.

A firm should treat its lawyers fairly and give everyone a fair shot. But assuming that it does, it sets the parameters a lawyer must have to sustain the firm in the years to come. If a young lawyer doesn't like what the firm requires or disagrees with the firm's values, they may give their input, but they cannot demand that the firm do things differently. What they can do is align and excel. Influence comes later. It's the employee who must align, and if that isn't possible, the lawyer may have to pivot to another practice and maybe even other work.

The challenge for every lawyer is to determine their values and align their conduct accordingly. And lawyers should do their best to find their place of service with others who are aligned with the same values they are. For some, that may be a specialized practice area, such as products-liability litigation at a large law firm, or it may be a small-firm practice representing plaintiffs in employment-discrimination cases. For others, it might mean joining a nonprofit organization or going to work for a judge or a criminal-defense firm. The process always begins with the lawyer first thinking about the kind of practice that is aligned with their values. Whatever the case may be, though, once the lawyer takes her position, she must commit to learning, growing, and becoming the most aligned lawyer she can.

Environmental Impact

My son Charles attended law school after getting a master's degree in accounting. He had taken a couple of business-law courses and thought a law degree would complement his accounting degree. I didn't necessarily agree, but Charles had grown up in the home of a lawyer, and if he was drawn to the practice, I'd let him explore the option. After all, he was an adult who was old enough to make his own choice. I left the law school decision to him, and he made the jump.

In his third year, Charles began trying cases under our state's student practice rule. One day he called to tell me that he was representing a defendant in an aggravated assault case. He would be assisted by a senior lawyer from the public defender's office, but he would be lead counsel at trial. The most experienced assistant district attorney in the county was prosecuting the case.

I talked with Charles from time to time during his trial preparation. He seemed in control and was making sound decisions, but I sensed he was stressed. The state's evidence was strong, but he had found a witness to the assault who was favorable to the defendant. He wasn't sure whether the testimony would be enough to overcome the state's evidence against him. Charles was convinced his client wasn't guilty of the charge.

When the trial was over, he called. I asked how he did, and he gave me the good news. He'd won. The witness he found testified that the victim started the fight and that the defendant was only defending himself against the attack. I told Charles it was difficult to get an acquittal, and that it was a pretty impressive result for a first trial against a seasoned prosecutor. I asked him what he'd learned about trial work and whether it was something he'd look for after graduation. He replied, "I learned if you prepare hard and do your best, you can be successful." He then added, "But I don't want to do this as a career."

Charles is just like so many other young attorneys I know. He had to experience trial work in order to know if it was a fit for him. Sometimes it is and sometimes it isn't, and if it isn't, a young attorney should make the sensible decision to look further for their fit. And just because Charles was not aligned with litigation work, just because the fit was not right, didn't mean he was a failure. It was not a comment on his work ethic, his character, or his value. It simply led him to pivot to a career he thought would be more fulfilling. It gave him the valuable data needed to evaluate his future. And knowing my son as I do, I would say he is much happier and much more fulfilled than he would have been had he chosen a life of litigation. He paid attention to the signals, the misalignment, and he made the right call.

Aligning your conduct and career to your personal values, passions, and the kind of work you love is important. It affects your personal relationships, your interactions with the courts and colleagues, and even your job satisfaction. But how do you evaluate whether or not you are an aligned lawyer? Let me give you a place to start.

Chapter 14

First Steps

"The very first step towards success in any occupation
is to become interested in it."
                    —*William Osler, physician and*
                    founder of Johns Hopkins Hospital

"Take time to deliberate; but when the time for action
arrives, stop thinking and go in."
                    —*Napoleon Bonaparte, French statesman*

One day, a lawyer I worked with on most of my cases walked
into the office and asked if I had a minute. She closed my door
and sat down. "I have a chance to join a federal agency and I
want your advice on whether I should take it." She was a spec-
tacular attorney. Lots of lawyers are smart and technically accomplished. Few really understand people, their motivations,
how to relate to them, and how to construct a practical strategy
for a case. This lawyer had all of these insights and skills, and
more. I hated that she was thinking about leaving.

I asked what interested her in the agency opportunity. It
was clear she had given the job a lot of thought. "I love it here,
but I want more responsibility, and I want my work to have more
impact." She continued: "I like hard, business-oriented cases,
and I've done a lot of that work with you, but I need work that
focuses on fairness and justice in commercial relationships and
transactions. The agency job has that focus," she said, and she

was willing to consider a reduction in salary for a change in her practice focus. These were the same things I had considered when I made changes in my career—moving from money-focused to value-focused work. I didn't want her to leave but my duty was to help her find alignment, and so I asked, "How can I help you?"

Interviewing Myself—To Step Down or Not Step Down

Alignment evaluation is a practice that's important throughout your career, and it's pretty fresh for me. I retired from the court on July 1, 2018. Several months before that date, I committed to a detailed analysis of my work on the court, my satisfaction with it, the environment in which I served, the value of remaining on the court, and whether continuing would materially improve citizen access to the court in our district. I asked myself how important my title and status were to me and whether remaining on the court with a reduced caseload would allow me to accomplish what I wanted in this season of my career. I asked: Could I contribute more elsewhere?

I created a list, outlining each of these issues. Reviewing it, I found my list centered more on my values than on any tangible, material benefit. The fact that federal judges receive a generous pension gave me the liberty to focus on the contribution I wanted to make and not the compensation it would produce. Still, I wasn't sure how to analyze what steps to take next.

I turned to Bob Lewis for advice. Bob is a close friend and an accomplished leadership and career consultant who founded Lewis Leadership. Over the years, Bob and I have had deep discussions about the work each of us was doing and where we wanted to have an impact. We talked about the importance of our marriages and the celebrations and struggles in our families. Simply put, he knows me well and knew that if I decided to retire, I would devote considerable time to meaningful work, paid or unpaid. He agreed to help me decide whether it was time to move on from the bench, and if I did, what "meaningful productive work" might look like in retirement.

Bob asked me to analyze my career as a federal judge and to distill what was and is important to me. Having served on the court for fourteen years, I had lots of data to draw on. During the first three years, everything was new, exciting, and interesting. I learned how to manage cases and watched lawyers litigate and try cases in ways different than I had seen before. In the middle years, I honed my skills as a judge. By then, there were few new kinds of cases, and I had enough experience to forecast how cases would play out and be resolved. Most cases were becoming rather routine. As I moved closer to retirement age, I found the work was less challenging. I also began to realize that a judge's work is almost wholly reactive. I was presiding over cases randomly assigned, responding to motions filed by the parties in the case, deciding issues the parties brought to me for consideration, and presiding over trials by managing evidence and lawyer trial conduct. I missed the freedom to initiate and innovate that I had in private practice and government service. A sense of freedom to innovate and close connection with people were missing from my work.

I shared my findings with Bob, and he said I was in the mastery phase of a work cycle—that is, work satisfaction was missing because I had mastered the work assigned. I valued difficult, challenging, and interesting cases, but the work had lost impact and importance, save for an occasional case randomly assigned that might have an impact on my community. Put simply, I wanted more to make more of a difference, and I concluded continuing to serve on the bench would not align with the values that now were important to me. I had completed my alignment analysis, and I knew it was time to move to something different.

Maybe you find yourself in a season like I was in. Maybe you're considering whether to continue in your present position or search for a job opportunity that aligns with your personal values and in this stage of your career. If so, let me give some thoughts about where you might begin your own alignment analysis.

Alignment Analysis

Alignment analysis at any stage of a profession begins with a serious consideration of one's values, beliefs, and priorities. A lawyer must also consider the shared values of the profession and the values of the firm or institution where she works. After all, these values should serve as the compass for professional and personal decisions.

Shared Professional Values

Each of us have taken oaths permitting us to practice. These oaths serve as the starting point for reminding lawyers of the shared values of the profession. But maybe you don't remember the oath you took. If not, the first step for the rediscovery of the shared values of our profession is to review it. These were, after all, the promises we made in return for the privilege to practice law.

As I described earlier, in my life I have taken oaths for public offices in which I've served. I've also taken oaths for admission to practice, one in South Carolina and the other in Georgia; two to practice in federal court in these two states; and one to practice before the United States Supreme Court. Each of these oaths were different. Some were longer than others, some more specific, but all constituted promises I made in serving as a lawyer.

Every alignment evaluation for a lawyer begins with rereading each of these oaths because they contain our sworn promises when we were authorized to practice law. I also suggest you read the Rules of Professional Conduct, because in many states you promise to abide by them when you swear your oath of admission. These codes are based on the ethical values·and conduct required to serve in our profession.

Because you made a solemn promise to abide by these shared professional values, they are not optional. They are a condition of being licensed to practice. So, if your values have changed, if you can no longer abide by the oaths you swore, you're no longer aligned for work within the legal field. If they have not changed, but you realize you've wandered from them, you need to start your return by recommitting to the shared values of our profession.

Personal Values

Determining your personal values might be a tougher task. Most people do not write their personal values down, and we likely didn't swear an oath to uphold them. Indeed, we may never have really defined what they are. What's more, personal values change over time as we experience life and obtain wisdom from it. Life changes and cultural influences have an effect on them. To discover one's values and to live by them takes courage, commitment, and conviction, which is critical in the aligning process, because defining what you value affects you and others.

When I was an associate at King & Spalding, we went to Dahlonega, Georgia, with friends for a weekend retreat. Seven or so married couples attended. I don't remember having any particular agenda, but I remember gathering on a Saturday morning at a picnic table. There, someone suggested that each person give the group one word that describes their spouse, and then explain why they chose their word. I remember the word Betsy used for me: honest. She shared examples, and then said my honesty was important to her and to our marriage.

I've thought over the years about that Saturday session and the word Betsy used to describe me. Honesty has been an important value for me in life and in my law practice. I remember times in my career when I needed to share hard and honest truths with clients or colleagues and had to think carefully about how best to communicate so my words would be considered. Aligning my practice to that value affected others and it affected my reputation. But there are numerous other personal values, many of which we don't consider. Some people value creativity, others want a collaborative work environment, and still others financial stability. And some values are more important than others. For instance, I valued honesty more than financial stability or personal success, and my commitment to honesty drove decisions on where and how to practice.

Have you done the hard work to identify the qualities and ideals most important to you? Many of us—and I include myself, during key parts of my life—have never made a list of what we value. The consequences of not doing so—consequences which I have suffered—include practicing values influenced by others, your environment, and the culture at large. These influences creep into and control lives. Truth be told, they've controlled mine from time to time.

So, how do you identify your values? I offer two suggestions. First, list them—all of them. Be honest in making the list. In making your list of values, include those you hold but wish you didn't. Why? Because they also influence your life and your practice and you may need to abandon them. It may also help you see whether your values are properly ordered, or whether a more negative value is preempting a more positive one. But don't just identify your values, examine whether you live by them.

Values affect our lives more directly than we acknowledge and more often than we'd like to admit. For example, many lawyers would say they value family, but there is a prevailing regret among lawyers about their capacity to serve and be present with their families. In my conversations with practitioners, more than one has said that they regret their time away from their children caused by the demands of work. I often ask them the same question I asked myself some years ago—when they prioritize work over their duties as a parent, to what value are they aligning? Are they aligning more to status or financial security than they are to the value of being a father, mother, husband, or wife? If so, why? And if so, how can you balance sustained financial success with personal matters important to you? Knowing your values allows you to examine whether your conduct aligns with what you claim is important. It allows you to recognize when you're choosing to engage in conduct that undercuts what you value most.

After you write down your values, consider discovering more about yourself and how you are wired, that is, what motivates, drives, and inspires you. This should not be specific to your work as a lawyer but should focus on understanding who you are as a person. I suggest you do two things. First, complete a personality assessment. You might take an Enneagram test, a StrengthsFinder exam, or a DiSC assessment. The Myers-Briggs Type Indicator must be administered by an MBTI-certified practitioner, but it comes with the benefit of an interpreter who can help you understand what the test shows. These kinds of assessments, while focusing on your personality type, also help identify what environment and activities you may prefer and in which you may excel, and how you relate to others, and how others relate to you. They might help you identify the kinds of careers and jobs that best allow you to be satisfied.

Finally, use your past experiences to identity your preferred alignment environment and activities. Take a sheet of paper and draw a line down the center. In the left column, list all the activities and experience in your life that were fulfilling and satisfying. Do not simply focus on law-related activities, and don't limit your list to experiences from your adult life. Simply list everything in your life that you've loved doing. If it was being on a Little League team, list it. If you like working on machines or cooking, list it. If you enjoy taking large volumes of information and organizing and prioritizing it, that goes on the list. If you enjoy traveling, or painting, or sitting in a quiet room reading or journaling, put it down. If you enjoy struggling with hard, heady issues or resolving conflict, jot these down also.

Now, in the right column, list those activities you didn't like. It may be monitoring your finances, or attending a cocktail party, or sitting in a lecture. Maybe it was speaking in public or hosting a meeting. It could be serving at youth events as an adult leader. List everything that didn't bring you joy or satisfaction.

When the lists are done, set them aside for a couple of days. Then find a quiet place and look first at the list of activities you liked, group them according to common characteristics, and then prioritize them according to how much you liked each category type. In the left column, you may have listed hosting a dinner, playing on an intramural team, or attending a men's conference. This grouping might indicate your preference for working in groups and collaborating with others. If you listed organizing document productions in a case or creating a flow chart for organizing an event in the left column, this might suggest you enjoy organizing activities and information so that they can be used productively.

Do the same grouping with the activities you don't like. When finished, list the environments and activities you found fulfilling and those you did not, and then compare them with your personality test to get a picture of what you like to do, where you like to do it, and whether it is consistent with your personality assessments.

Finally, I suggest you complete the Personal Goal Evaluation below. My friend Bob Lewis developed this series of questions. It is useful in a lawyer's alignment analysis, and it will help you envision how you might live and practice in an aligned way. It can help you identify the barriers to alignment, too. The questions are ordered untraditionally, beginning with goals that are important, but not urgent, and which get overlooked or ignored when we typically evaluate career and life decisions.

The Personal Goal Evaluation

1. **Spiritual and Philosophical** (care of the human spirit individually and in community)
   What is my overarching goal—what do I want to achieve in this area of my life?
   What does success look like—when I attain this goal what will I and others experience?
   Barriers to success—what will or could interfere with success?

2. **Relational** (marriage, family, colleagues, friends)
   What is my overarching goal—what do I want to achieve in this area of my life?
   What does success look like—when I attain this goal what will I and others experience?
   Barriers to success—what will or could interfere with success?

3. **Personal** (interests, avocations, wellness, activities)
   What is my overarching goal—what do I want to achieve in this area of my life?
   What does success look like—when I attain this goal what will I and others experience?
   Barriers to success—what will or could interfere with success?

4. **Community** (impact on organizations or community)
   What is my overarching goal—what do I want to achieve in this area of my life?
   What does success look like—when I attain this goal what will I and others experience?
   Barriers to success—what will or could interfere with success?

5. **Financial** (personal, charitable, family, education)
   What is my overarching goal—what do I want to achieve in this area of my life?
   What does success look like—when I attain this goal what will I and others experience?
   Barriers to success—what will or could interfere with success?

6. **Professional** (career, reputation, stature)
   What is my overarching goal—what do I want to achieve in this area of my life?
   What does success look like—when I attain this goal what will I and others experience?
   Barriers to success—what will or could interfere with success?

These questions are challenging, and they may take time. To be useful, though, the power of this exercise is in ordering the six categories by priority. Your order may be different than the order in which they are listed above. How you order them will tell you a lot. This ordering process will require some soul-searching and require you to be honest with yourself. The end result may be an important guide in deciding what, where, and how you will practice law, or whether you will practice at all.

Testing My Own Personal Goal Evaluation

Bob Lewis tested the conclusions I reached about my values and what alignment looked like in retirement. These exercises, together with Bob's input and the input of a couple of other trusted confidants, were influential in organizing my thoughts and provided a framework for evaluating my decision. Only after struggling with the issue of what was next in my career and life, and reaching some tentative conclusions, did I have a final meeting with the person who knew me best, the person who could test if

I had done the evaluation and reached conclusions honestly and completely—my wife, Betsy. Before we talked, Betsy completed the goals exercise by answering the questions based on what she considered my primary goals and objectives, and based on what she knew and had seen of me. I wanted her to tell me what she thought I valued most and what work she thought would align best with those values. And she was entitled to input because my decision affected the alignment in her life. She shared her own analysis: it was time for me to move on. And so, after completing my own alignment analysis and speaking with Betsy, I chose to move to different work with different objectives.

After making my decision to retire, I shared it with Dwight Davis. Dwight is one of my dearest friends and confidants. He's a likable guy and a remarkable lawyer. About the same age, Dwight retired a couple of years before me. When I shared with him confidentially that I had decided to step down from the court, he said, "That doesn't surprise me. Judge Bell used to tell us that we needed to remake ourselves every fifteen years." Judge Bell was always investing in us by offering principles with which to guide our lives. He did that until his death nine years ago. Our last visit with him was poignant because even near death, Judge Bell was investing in our lives.

Knowing his life was nearing an end, Dwight, Doc Schneider (another close friend), and I visited Judge Griffin B. Bell at his home in Americus, Georgia. The three of us had been his protégées and his law partners. Although he spent most of his adult years in Atlanta, Americus is where he was born and where his character and values were instilled. It was fitting that he would choose to return there to spend the final weeks of his life.

In the years we knew him, and even in his house that January, Judge Bell told us we should leave Atlanta and move to Newton or some other small, more rural town. His mantra was to live far enough from Atlanta to enable us to live life without the demands and distractions of a big city. He wanted us to find our Americus, a place where we could discover and share our values. He mentored us, even to the end.

On the day we visited Americus, we devoted our time to reminiscing about our shared experiences, cases we handled together, our law firm and its partners, and our hopes. We shared how important he was to us. It was a way for all of us to finish a friendship well. Near the end of our time together, he paused, then said, "I have lived a great life and loved being a lawyer. I am ready to go."

I'm convinced Judge Bell told us he was ready in order to comfort us. But he also shared it because it was true. That was the kind of man he was over the thirty or so years we knew him—always serving others. Those who knew him as well as we did acknowledged the influence he had on the way we practiced. He influenced us by what he said and how he lived. While he was alive, Judge Bell's values were always on display—his deep devotion to the family he loved, the friends he cherished, the country he served, the clients he represented, the firm at which he spent so much of his professional life, and his love of being a lawyer. Whether in private or public practice, he served the profession with honor and dignity. He wanted that for us—to know the joy of living life aligned.

Do the Work, Benefit from the Results

Now, about the woman I told you about in the beginning of this chapter who was considering leaving the firm for a federal agency position. After the meeting in my office, we talked several times about public service, the agency job she was considering, and how her career would be affected if she decided not to pivot to other work. We also talked about what she wanted to accomplish personally—in her marriage, the family she wanted to have, her desire to find ways to contribute to her community and to have balance in her life.

I also arranged for her to talk to other lawyers who had worked or were working in public service jobs and not just rely on my opinions. I was with her during one of these meetings. This one with Judge Bell. He had never met her, but that didn't matter. She wanted wisdom, and he was always available to talk to young attorneys. They talked for a while about her public service opportunity. At the end of the conversation, he summed up his advice by telling her this: "If you stay here, you will work on some of the interesting cases in the country, you will work with some of the best lawyers in the country, and you will earn an income beyond what you can image. If you stay, someday when you are old, and you have your grandchildren on you knee, you can tell them that you had about a C+ life." His point: she needed to find where she was called to serve in the profession. And this required taking the risk to do different work to find where she truly fit. She took the federal job. I mourned her loss but relish that she decided to take a chance on something new.

Here's one last story. Remember Joann, the young lawyer who thought she might lose her position when her law firm merged with another firm? The lawyer who wanted to stay in the legal profession but looked at pivoting to marketing work for a law firm? That was a couple of years ago, and she continued to do legal work after failing to get the legal marketing position. But she also kept on analyzing where she fit. How do I know? Because a few days ago I received an email from her. I'm going to quote from it. You draw your own conclusions about the value of alignment: "The marketing position at that firm didn't work out, which led to me accepting a short position at a small firm.... I left there and ended up doing contract work for almost two years to keep practicing law and stay afloat. That was obviously stressful...but I wasn't finding any positions I was really interested in. Then 2020 happened, of course." But Joann didn't give up and got word of a job opening at the firm where a friend worked. She applied and was hired during her interview. I know the firm she joined—a small, well-respected specialty practice. Here is what she said about it:

> I'm now practicing family law (plot twist) at [name of firm]. I'm loving it. I never thought I'd love family law, but here I am. The first four years of practicing law I felt completely lost and very unhappy—almost decided to switch fields. I'm glad I didn't because this is the first job practicing law that I feel like fits me. I get to write all day, every day, which I'm sure you recall was something I wanted. Everyone here is lovely to work with, and it's a great firm atmosphere where the partners all want to teach and allow you to grow as an attorney—what I think is hard to find and other young attorney friends agree.
>
> So, all that being said, I'm really blessed to have this position.... I do my best every day and actually don't dread going to work. I feel like I'm actually getting to help people through one of the most difficult times in their life, which was important to me to feel fulfilled.
> —Email dated April 9, 2021

Amen. An aligned lawyer who discovered her significance.

Some Final Thoughts

Practicing law is a privilege, and serving others by helping them with your legal expertise is satisfying beyond measure if your practice is aligned.

Alignment does not happen serendipitously. It is the product of hard work, commitment, and honesty with yourself. I've done the work to find alignment and have course corrected when I've fallen out of it. And even now I'm finding fulfilment in satisfying work in my new season of life. I get to write about our profession, about how to seek fulfilment in aligned practices. I have the privilege to meet with young lawyers who seek to pivot in their careers. I consult with clients and law firms about their cases, and I share with them honestly and authentically how principled and reasoned positions can result in just and fair outcomes. And better yet, I'm doing a bit more road biking.

There is fulfilment in having a legal career that's aligned with your core values. There's satisfaction in knowing you're pursuing your passion and purpose with authenticity. My hope is that you've already found this kind of alignment. But if you haven't, I hope you'll do the work to find it. Go out and align your practice with the values of the profession and the values personal to you. Don't let your alignment be thrown out of whack by the demands of your clients, your firm, or the expectations placed on lawyers by colleagues or culture. Be true to your values. Fight for your purpose. Be relentless. Finish well.

Acknowledgments

This section is entitled "Acknowledgments," the traditional heading for this part of the book. But "Grateful" is the better word. This book was in the making for all forty-five years of my professional life. I practiced with remarkable lawyers, and their example and professionalism are represented on these pages. I am indebted to Griffin B. Bell, Frank Jones, Bob Fiske, and Ken Starr for their investment in my life. I am thankful for Doc Schneider's and Dwight Davis's example and friendship and their encouragement for me to write.

I am grateful to Marc Jolley and Mercer University Press for their willingness to publish and to Mary Pearson, editor extraordinaire. Thanks to Sealy Yates, who ably served as my agent, and to Seth Haines for his review and suggestions on the manuscript. I am grateful for their encouragement about the message of the book and its need in our profession.

To my sons, Charles and Scott, your support in all my professional wanderings and musings means a lot to me.

Most of all, I am grateful for Betsy. She believed in what I was writing and believed in me. As an author herself, she modeled the discipline it takes to write and the humility needed to accept criticism.

For those whose stories are told in this book, thank you for the illustrations that helped me make my points about our profession. Thanks to all with whom I have practiced and those who served in the offices where I worked. Finally, thanks to all of those who have trusted me to represent you, and I am grateful to my country for the opportunity to serve the public in four different public offices.